HOW TO WRITE A POEM

BY MARGARET RYAN

A SPEAK OUT, WRITE ON! BOOK
Franklin Watts
A Division of Grolier Publishing
New York / London / Hong Kong / Sydney
Danbury, Connecticut

Photo credits ©: AP/Wide World Photos: 46; Archive Photos: 115;
Art Resource: 14; Bettmann Archive: 62, 107, 140; Books & Co.: 176;
Brown Brothers: 88; Comstock: 11 (Sven Martson), 26 (Sven Martson),
168 (Sven Martson); Photo Researchers: 35, 37 (Lowell Georgia);
Photri Inc.: 29 (Robert Ginn); UPI/Corbis-Bettmann: 129.

For permissions for quoted materials see page 190.

Library of Congress Cataloging-in-Publication Data

Ryan, Margaret.
How to write a poem / by Margaret Ryan.
p.   cm. — (Speak out, write on!)
Includes bibliographical references and index.
ISBN 0-531-11252-7 (lib. bdg.)   ISBN 0-531-15788-1 (pbk.)
1. Poetry—Authorship. I. Title II. Series: Speak out, write on! book.
PN1059.A9R93 1996
808.1—dc20   96-12095
                                                         CIP AC

HOW TO WRITE A POEM

INTRODUCTION

For the discussion of the drafts of Elizabeth Bishop's poem "One Art," as well as a list of rhyme words EB used in drafting an earlier, unfinished villanelle ("The Aviary"), I am indebted to *Elizabeth Bishop: Life and the Memory of It*, by Brett C. Miller, University of California Press, Berkeley, California, 1993.

Poems used as examples and not otherwise credited are the works of the author.

CONTENTS

ONE
HOW TO WRITE
A POEM

*I have a feeling that verse exists before
it is composed.*
—Nadezhda Mandelstam

There is no one way to write a poem. Nor is there a magic formula or process that, when followed precisely, will automatically transform a series of words into poetry. Creating poetry is personal—a private act that draws upon your thoughts, your feelings, your knowledge of people and your knowledge of language. Unlike cars or computers, poems cannot be mass-produced.

On the contrary, each poem is written in its own way. Some poems emerge almost fully composed, demanding only to be transposed from your imagination onto paper. Others suggest themselves more subtly, with the merest hint of their sound, their subject, or their mood. Sometimes a single word, a line, or a stanza seems to be given to the poet, who then must painstakingly track down the rest. Still other poems, like shy guests, must be coaxed gently and persistently out of corners and shadows and patiently be wooed into finally appearing as a series of words printed on a page.

Writing a poem is obviously different from solving a math equation or performing a chemistry experiment. It's not a precise process that can be repeated at any time, or by any person, with the same results. Still, it is possible to sketch the process by which poems are made.

THE PROCESS OF WRITING A POEM

First, there's the impulse to write, wherever it comes from. It might be a strong feeling—love, anger, grief—that demands expression. It could be an assignment from a teacher, complete with a deadline—so you know you must write a poem between now and Friday. Or you might be inspired by a sense of playful curiosity (let's see if I can do this…), or by a line or phrase that haunts you and insists upon being written down. You might be inspired by another poem.

Whatever gets you started, that initial impulse leads to a first draft. The draft may be a journal entry, a few notes on the back of an envelope or an index card, a couple of rambling paragraphs of description, or a fully formed sonnet carefully written out on a sheet of lined paper.

Many poems get no further than this. The assignment is dashed off and handed in; the scene or saying is noted in a few words; the envelope or index card is stuffed into a pocket, left on a dresser, or disappears into a drawer. Once the thought or feeling has been fastened down in words, the writer never thinks of it, or works with it, again.

Most good poetry is the product of strenuous work and several revisions.

THE FACT OF REVISION

Most poetic impulses that make their way into full-blown poems, however, will undergo another look—a revision. In fact, they will probably go through many revisions before the poem is completed, or abandoned. When a poem is well made, the effort that went into creating it does not show. We hear, in the best poems, the song or the speech of humanity; we do not see or hear the struggle of producing it.

What happens during revision? The poet might tinker with the order of the words, add sensuous detail, or cut extraneous words and abstract phrases. The poet might play with the shape of the poem, rearranging words on the page. Or the poet could notice certain sound patterns within the lines and decide to highlight their effect, or minimize it.

Sometimes the changes a poet makes in revision are minor—a word here or there, a line break. Other times, the changes are major. Last lines become first lines. The writer changes many words to move the language closer to his or her true feelings. Sometimes, even the message of the poem—what it says—changes, as the poem eventually states the very opposite of what the poet wrote in early drafts.

Most successful poems—the ones you read in magazines or anthologies, the ones you remember or turn to as old friends—have been revised many times. But even poets themselves can forget how hard they worked once the poem is completed. It's similar to the way a mother might forget the difficulties of childbirth once her beautiful infant has arrived.

Take the case of poet Elizabeth Bishop, for example. An interviewer asked her if she'd ever written a poem easily, if any poems came to her as gifts. Bishop replied that she had written a villanelle, a French poetic form of nineteen lines divided into six stanzas, that way. "It was just like writing a letter," she said.

In fact, seventeen drafts of this villanelle, titled "One Art," exist. They show that Bishop started with some rough notes and an idea. Next, she began composing lines that set the rhyme scheme in place. She tinkered with the closing lines extensively, and finally the poem came to completion. If it took seventeen drafts to write a poem that came so easily, imagine how many drafts other Bishop poems went through!

Some poets labor months or years on a single poem. Another Bishop poem, "The Moose," was twenty years in the writing. Although she had the beginning stanzas and the end, Bishop said she just couldn't get from one place to the other. She kept working on it, however, and eventually finished and published the poem.

THE NEED FOR PATIENCE

Why can it take so long to write a poem? There are several reasons. For one thing, it always takes longer to write something short, compact, accurate, and concise than it does to write something rambling and long-winded. Or as the philosopher Blaise Pascal once wrote to a friend, "If I had more time, I would have written you a shorter letter."

Poetry, by its nature, is compact, condensed, and concentrated. As Ezra Pound wrote in *The ABC of Reading*, "Poetry consists of gists and piths." He went on to insist that poetry "is not something 'more wafty and imbecile' than prose, but something charged to a higher potential." Poetry is not watered-down prose, he continues, but "the most concentrated form of verbal expression."

A contemporary poet, John Drury, says that

*The poet, translator, and critic Ezra Pound was a
tremendous influence on twentieth century poetry.*

poetry is language that has been "condensed, com-
pacted, tightened and trimmed." It takes time for a
writer to determine what to remove from a poem without harming it, and where the essence of the poem—
the untouchable elements—lies.

Although revision shouldn't be rushed, there are ways to speed it up a bit. Having other people read your work, offer suggestions, and give you their reactions can make the job go faster.

Still, it often takes longer to write a short poem than anyone—other than another poet—would suppose. In his autobiography, the poet W. B. Yeats wrote about the difficulty of the work: "Nothing is done upon the first day, not one rhyme is in place; and when at last the rhymes begin to come, the first rough draft of a six line stanza takes the whole day."

Another poet, Ranier Maria Rilke, discussed the need for patience in his book *Letters to a Young Poet*. Rilke wrote:

> *Being an artist means, not reckoning and counting, but ripening like the tree which does not force its sap and stands confident in the storms of spring without the fear that after them may come no summer. It does come. But it comes only to the patient...patience is everything.*

WRITING AS REVELATION

It can take so long to write a poem for another reason: in writing poetry, we reveal ourselves. Because most people know themselves imperfectly at best, this makes the process challenging. Very few of us have the gift that poet Robert Burns defined in his "Ode to a Louse": to see ourselves as others see us. We are complex creatures, and we are often so busy *being* ourselves we can't really *see* ourselves.

Then, of course, who we are—what we think about a certain subject, how we feel—physically, mentally, emotionally—is constantly changing. We change over time and through experience.

Though getting to know oneself is not easy, poetry is a way to learn what we think and feel. Poems can serve as mirrors, or as X rays, giving us snapshots of who we are inside and of how we think and feel at a given moment. In the process of writing poetry, we can discover ourselves.

GETTING TO THE TRUTH

Discovering oneself is not necessarily a pleasant process. Although an old saying asserts, "The truth will set you free," another aphorism insists, "The truth hurts." Many people find themselves blocked in their attempt to write poetry because they are afraid of discovering who they are and what they really feel.

What if you don't like the self you discover? What if you discover a self that's disorderly, disobedient, rude, quick-tempered, bitter, or possessed of some other awful qualities? What if you find you really do hate your brother, that you think school is truly boring, that you actually do want to run away and join the circus?

Welcome to the human race. The fact is, no one's perfect. And which would you prefer: to learn your feelings about your siblings through writing a poem or to discover them as you whack them over the head with a two-by-four?

Learning about yourself through imagination is safer, and easier, than learning through acting out. Poetry, and all imaginative work, allows you to "live" events, and "have" experiences that might be unsafe or dangerous to have in fact. Poetry, then, is a kind of virtual reality, where you can explore feelings, posit what-ifs, and see what happens.

If you discover something you don't like about yourself, you never have to share that knowledge—or the poem—with anyone else. You never have to act on what you learn—although there may be times when the insights you gain about yourself through writing can lead to a little self-improvement.

THE TRADITION

Poetry can be a path toward self-knowledge and a means of exploration. But poetry is not the same as self-expression, and it's more than a personal activity.

Poetry also plays a cultural role. As the widow of the Russian poet Osip Mandelstam wrote:

> The work of the poet, as a vehicle for world harmony, has a social character—that is, it is concerned with the doings of the poet's fellow men, among whom he lives and whose fate he shares. He does not speak "for them," but with them, nor does he set himself apart from them: otherwise he would not be a source of truth.

Through poetry, we learn how to be human, how to deal with suffering, what is important and lasting, and what really doesn't matter much.

As a cultural activity, poetry has a life of its own. Individual poets contribute to it, but the tradition flows like a river through human experience. It has a history, a current state of being, and—with any luck—a future. When you write poetry, you are taking your place in the procession of poets who have gone before you, those writing now, and those who will come after you. You are taking part in the conversation of poetry that stretches back to before the existence of the written alphabet and that continues in every nation and in every language.

CONVENTIONS

Have you ever thought about the ways in which artists render distance or create the illusion of three dimensions on a flat piece of paper? The system that's used is called perspective, and it involves such conventions as making objects in the distance smaller than those nearby and using parallel lines that converge toward a vanishing point. The rules that govern perspective drawing became universal in Europe during the fourteenth century. They are essentially a set of agreements, or conventions, on which Western artists and viewers agree.

Language has conventions. For instance, in English, we agree that adding an s to the end of a noun means the word stands for more than one of the item we're naming (tree or trees). We have even agreed that the word "tree" can represent a whole class of things—including maples, birches, elms, and oaks—but not including roses or daisies.

Poetry has its conventions, too. There are agreed-upon ways of communicating, a kind of shorthand, that poets and readers both accept and expect. These conventions change as certain ideas and styles come into and go out of fashion. There have been times when no serious poet would write without rhyme, for example, and other times when no serious poet would dare to use it. Sometimes traditional forms are the trend; everyone writes in couplets or composes sonnets. At other times, the tendency is away from rules and restrictions, and being "free" is the order of the day.

This is not to say that your poetry must follow the fashion of the times, only that it's helpful to know what's fashionable today and what other tools and techniques from different ages are available to you. When free verse was all the rage, American poet Robert Frost compared writing it to "playing tennis with the net down," and continued to write in conventional meters, to work in full sentences, and to use rhyme to great advantage—even though it wasn't fashionable.

Learning to handle the conventions of poetry is like learning to use a saw, a plane, and a hammer if you want to be a carpenter. Rhyme, meter, form, similes, and metaphors are tools that poets use to construct their works. And knowing how to use them, and when to use them—or not—will give you more range and greater possibilities of expression. These tools can make it easier to say—to write—what's in your heart.

In fact, learning those rules, and playing with them, can provide a great deal of pleasure. It may even be the sign that you really are a poet. As W. H. Auden remarked in an interview:

> I can't understand—strictly from a hedonistic point of view—how one can enjoy writing with no form at all. If one plays a game, one needs rules. Otherwise, there is no fun.

Auden also quotes French poet Paul Valéry, who said that a person is a poet if his or her imagination is stimulated by the difficulties inherent in his or her art—and not if his or her imagination is dulled by them.

STARTING OUT

In poetry, you are always at the beginning. You are always starting again because, even if you've written a thousand poems, the next one is a different experience. Each presents its own set of challenges: a different subject, a different form, a different time, a different you.

Still, there are some ways to approach the writing of poetry that can help you get started. And there are ways of looking at poems you've already written—as if through a series of lenses—that can help you to rewrite, revise, and refine the draft of a poem that already exists.

In this book, you will find suggestions on how to get ready to write, how to pick a subject, and how to produce a first draft. You'll also find detailed information on how to revise a draft from a number of points of view. In fact, because most writing is rewriting, most of the chapters will deal with revision. Each will give you a different way to look at your first draft and to think about changing and improving it. You'll also find suggestions throughout the book on using revision techniques to begin new poems.

But before you begin, here are two warnings: First, writing about it—or talking about it—is much easier than doing it. Writing poetry takes time, effort, intelligence, and compassion. It will draw on many of your intellectual, emotional, and artistic powers. So please don't be surprised—or disappointed—if you're not dashing off dazzling sonnets every other day.

Second, because there are as many ways of writing poems as there are people and poems, no book can offer a foolproof formula. There is no complete manual. Those who have experience in writing poetry can share hints, suggestions, and advice. But the stuff of poetry—imagination, ideas, dreams, feelings, thoughts, words, and music—must come from you.

TWO

$\mathscr{P}$REPARING TO WRITE

A poem records emotions and moods that lie
beyond normal language...
—Diane Ackerman

Few people would dream of entering a marathon without first learning what it is: a footrace of about twenty-six miles. Once that was known, most would-be marathon runners would still give the ordeal some careful thought and might then undertake an extensive period of training.

Those who want to—or have to—write a poem would likewise do well to understand what they're getting into and begin by getting in shape.

DEFINING POETRY

Do you need to know what a poem is before you set out to write one? It would help. Unfortunately, to date, there is no single definition that clearly and simply defines poetry to everyone's satisfaction. Poetry, like magic and miracles, is hard to pin down, and many poets have an easier time saying what poetry is not than what it is.

In Carol Shields's novel *Swann*, however, one of her characters offers a definition of poetry that is fairly complete and compelling:

> *The impertinent human wish to reach into the sea of common language and extract from it the rich dark beautiful words that could be arranged in such a way that the unsayable might be said.*

Poetry speaks of the other life, the one we try to smother and forget.

POETRY—NOT PROSE

Many poets who try to define poetry begin by making a distinction between poetry and prose. Samuel Taylor Coleridge, for example, called prose "words in their best order," and poetry "the best words in their best order." Coleridge also defined poetry as "that species of composition which is opposed to the work of science," because poetry proposes to give pleasure first and then to supply truth. Ezra Pound drew the distinction between the two genres by noting that one reads prose for the subject matter and poetry for something else.

Even our greatest writers cannot precisely say where the boundary between poetry and prose lies. The Russian novelist Leo Tolstoy said, "The question is raised in manuals of style, yet the answer to it lies beyond me." He suggested that poetry might be "everything with the exception of business documents and school books."

In the original version of her poem "Poetry," however, American poet Marianne Moore disputes

Tolstoy, writing that it isn't fair to discriminate against certain kinds of documents.

Moore believes it's how a poet handles certain material, not the material itself, that makes the difference between poetry and prose.

RECOGNIZING POETRY

Poet Richard Howard noted that "prose proceeds, verse reverses." Perhaps the first thing you notice about poetry is that it looks different on the page from prose. Prose proceeds to the end of the line, then wraps around to the next one. Poetry, on the other hand, stops not at the far right margin, but where the poet decides a line should end. Verse "turns the corner," giving the poet control over the arrangement of the words on a page. In fact, the shape of those words, and the choice of where a line ends, can be a significant element of a poem's meaning.

But there's more to poetry than the fact that it looks different from prose. And it's not only that lots of poetry rhymes. Commercial jingles and greeting-card verses rhyme, too, but these are not poetry.

Samuel Johnson called poetry the art of combining pleasure with truth. Robert Frost wrote that "a poem begins in delight and ends in wisdom." By his definition, then, poetry should give pleasure and provide insight. In this, Frost agrees with the poet of ancient Rome, Horace, who declared that poetry must be *dulce et utile*, both beautiful and useful.

William Wordsworth's definition of poetry—"the spontaneous overflow of powerful feelings...recollected in tranquility"—is widely known and often quoted. Less known, but equally apt, is Paul Fussell's definition: "The art of poetry is the art of knowing language and people equally well."

Some poets—and critics—dispute Fussell's definition. They think that poetry is really all about itself; that is to say, about language. Yet it is difficult to ignore the importance of feeling and emotion in poetry.

THE REALITY OF FEELING

Human emotion occurs in time and space, within our physical bodies. We feel things in our flesh: pain, joy, nervousness, and elation manifest themselves within the body. Poetry, in conveying information about feelings, helps us understand what it means to be human. One of the benefits of writing poetry is that you will know and understand your own feelings better.

To convey feelings, poetry often uses words that appeal to one of the five senses: sight, hearing, smell, touch, and taste. And poetry makes use of the music inherent in language, emphasizing rhythms or working with the sound of words to recreate a feeling in the listener.

In a letter, Emily Dickinson defined poetry based solely on the way it made her feel:

> If I read a book and it makes my whole body so cold no fire can ever warm me, I know that is poetry. If I feel physically as if the top of my head were taken off, I know that is poetry. These are the only ways I know it. Is there any other way?

How do you feel when you've read a poem? What physical response lets you recognize a real poem every time? You might spend some time thinking about how you'd like a reader to feel after reading one of your poems, too. Keep this in mind as you write and make it your ideal to recreate that feeling.

READING AND LISTENING

"Anyone wanting to know about poetry would do one of two things, or both," Ezra Pound wrote in *The ABC of Reading*, "i.e., look at it or listen to it."

If you want to write poetry—or even if you just *have* to write poetry to fulfill the requirements of a course—then you must read poetry. You wouldn't expect to become a filmmaker without ever going to the movies, would you? And who would dream of composing without ever listening to music?

Immerse yourself in poetry. Study the plays of Shakespeare. Read Chaucer. Absorb John Donne and Wyatt and Surrey and Spenser. Read contemporary poets, too. As George G. Elliott stated: "Read around. Read promiscuously." Expand your scope by reading various selections in poetry anthologies. Try both classic compilations, such as *The Norton Anthology of Poetry*, and contemporary collections, such as the paperback series *Best Poems* of a particular year.

If you know a foreign language, read poetry in that language. You might also read poems in translation, such as the work of Nazim Hikmet, a Turkish poet, or the work of some of the great Russian poets, such as Anna Akhmatova and Osip Mandelstam, or the German poet Ranier Maria Rilke.

Of course, when reading poetry in translation, you will miss a great deal of what made the original text poetic—the music, the sound of the original language, the poet's choice of one word over another. Still, reading translations can give you an excellent sense of the subjects other poets have chosen to write about.

You might also look at modern literary magazines, such as *Poetry*, the *Paris Review*, *Mudfish*, and *Boulevard*. Sample some poems from more general

Your local library is an excellent resource for books and recordings of poetry.

publications, such as the *New Yorker*, the *New Republic*, or the *Atlantic*.

To listen to poetry, start reading it aloud to yourself. Read your favorite poems to friends or family members, and have them read their favorites to you. Borrow recordings of poets reading their own works from the library. You might enjoy attending a poetry reading at a local bookstore, a coffeehouse, a college campus, or at a local church or high school, to get a sense of how a particular poet's voice sounds.

You will find, when you begin to read and listen to poetry, that people differ about what poetry is, how it should look on the page, and what poems should be about. Eventually, you will have to decide what makes something a poem—and what you'd like your poems to look like, to say, and to do. Reading and listening will help you discover what poetry is for you.

WARMING UP

If you read many books about writing, you'll find remarkable agreement on one point: Everyone who really wants to write—whether poetry, prose, or drama—should write freely and often, preferably every day.

Dorothea Brande, in *Becoming a Writer*, urges beginners to rise half an hour earlier than usual, and "just as you rise, begin to write. Write anything that comes into your head. You are training yourself simply to write." She urges that you write as long as you have time or until you feel you have written yourself out.

In addition, Brande encourages writers to determine, within a day or two, the number of words they can write in one sitting. Once you've found this limit, push it ahead by a few lines or a few sentences until you have doubled your output.

While Brande—and others—measure a day's work in words or lines, writing coach Natalie Goldberg claims in *Writing Down the Bones* that the basic unit of writing is the timed practice. It can be ten minutes, twenty minutes, or an hour. Like Brande,

Goldberg suggests that you gradually work up to longer sessions. Goldberg's rules include: keep your hand moving; don't cross out; lose control. She calls her method "the practice school of writing. The more you do it, the better you get at it."

In *If You Want to Write*, Brenda Ueland first offers encouragement: "Everyone is talented, original, and has something to say." Soon, she is giving advice about writing: "Creative work...is like a faucet: nothing comes unless you turn it on, and the more you turn it on, the more it comes."

She also encourages writers to keep a journal: "Write every day, or as often as you possibly can, as fast and carelessly as you possibly can, without reading it again, anything you happened to have thought, seen, or felt the day before." In six months, she urges, begin to look at this freewriting you've done. "A drawer full of paper will have accumulated. You will see that what you have written with slovenly freedom—in those parts there will be vitality, brilliance, beauty."

Writers give similar advice in classes. In a weekend poetry-writing workshop, poet Carolyn Forché told her class to write meditatively every day. She urged using the pen as if it were a light searching through the darkness to find the truth.

Although there are some poets who form their work entirely in their imaginations before they commit a word to paper, there are many others for whom practice writing, or freewriting, is essential. It lets them loosen up and makes them comfortable playing with words. You have nothing to lose by giving this kind of freewriting a try.

Don't worry about making sense, writing everything you did yesterday, or everything you have on your list for today. Get the juices flowing, get the muscles working that will produce poems. Write for

*Inspiration to write in a journal can strike you
at any time in the day.*

a specified time or for a certain number of pages. Twenty minutes at a stretch, or three pages, are achievable goals.

Don't show these pages to anyone, or even look at them for a while. After you've written freely for at least two weeks, you can go back to read what you've written. Underline strong passages and copy them over or type them up. You will certainly discover some interesting writing—including the seeds of many poems, and perhaps a few whole poems.

FREEWRITING INTO POEMS

Many writers use freewriting sessions to begin new work. Because poetry is condensed and compact by nature, you will need to concentrate what you've scrawled out and give some shape to it.

Begin by reading your freewriting, underlining the parts that have power for you. Listen for your own voice in the writing. What sounds original—or most like you? Look for strong images—visual pictures, descriptions that are concise and strike you as accurate. You may find passages of a story you've begun to note down. Occasionally, you'll find a complete or almost complete poem.

Copy the passages that strike you as having power or magic onto clean sheets of paper. Now read over what you've culled out, and put the pages aside again.

In a few days or a week, take out the reduced freewriting. Read through it once more. Underline or circle the strongest passages and edit out the language that, by comparison, seems dull.

Keep at this process, and you will begin to see poems—or notes for poems—emerging. You might find a few lines that you decide to lift out of the freewriting, add to, and work into a poem. As sections begin to appear distinct, copy them onto separate pieces of paper. You could start a file folder to hold each of your works in progress as they grow and separate from the main flow of your work.

SOME ADDITIONAL ADVICE

In a recent issue of *Poets and Writers* magazine, Irish poet Eavan Boland wrote about her methods of surviving as a poet. Her advice includes writing in a notebook and keeping that notebook visible, ready for the next day's work. She learned, she says, to date the pages. She also suggests thinking about what you've written as you go about the other tasks of your day. You may find it helpful to reflect upon your work as you're walking to school, driving in the car, or doing chores.

Why think about poems when you aren't actually writing them? It's all part of getting into condition to write well. Few people get brilliant ideas about things they don't consider seriously. If you never think about Fermat's last theorem or nuclear fission, for instance, you are unlikely to have insights about them.

Few poets (unless they are also physicists) have brilliant insights into rocket science. But many receive insights into their own work, and other gifts—words, phrases, lines, even whole stanzas—can come to them as if from some invisible source of poetry, just as they are folding clothes, or walking the dog, or weeding the garden.

The important thing is to listen. As Mandelstam's widow wrote:

> Many poets have said that a poem begins with a musical phrase ringing insistently in their ears; at first inchoate, it later takes on a precise form, although still without words.... At some point words formed behind the musical phrase and then the lips began to move.... The whole process of composition is one of straining to catch and record something compounded of harmony and sense as it is relayed from an unknown source and gradually forms itself into words.

If you almost constantly think about poems, read poems, and listen for the music of language, you are much more likely to receive these gifts and put them to use.

THREE

FINDING A SUBJECT

*A poet needs a subject the way a bricklayer
needs a brick.*
                    —Lawrence Jay Dessner

When you set out to write anything—a poem, a short story, an essay, or even a song—you need something to write about. You need material: some thing, or person, or place on which to focus your attention. You need to limit the area in which you're working and make it easier to create an object made of words.

Even a brief glance at the table of contents of a poetry anthology shows how many topics are the possible stuff of poetry. *The Best Poems of 1994*, for example, included among others poems with the following titles:

"A Short History of the Vietnam War Years"
"Cinema Verité"
"Myrtle"
"Tremendous Mood Swings"
"What You Want Means What You Can Afford"

"Demographics"
"A Catalpa Tree on West 12th Street"
"Life Drawing"
"Bulimia"
"The Frog in the Swimming Pool"
"Baseball"
"The Foot"
"Contempt"
"I Was on a Golf Course the Day John Cage Died of a Stroke"

Sports, eating disorders, cityscapes, feelings—these are all the stuff of poetry because they are all part of life. And as the poet Archibald MacLeish said, "The subject of art is life. You learn life by living it."

Don't worry that there's nothing left to write about, that all the good topics have been taken. In a way, of course, they have; unless something has just been invented or discovered, there's probably already at least one poem about it.

On the other hand, it's not so much the subject of the poem that makes it special; rather it's the way you write about that subject, the language you choose, your insights, your feelings, and your point of view that really matter. "Old wine in new bottles," the ancients used to say, meaning it's how you package your thoughts that matters. Ezra Pound's motto was: "Make it new."

WHAT MATTERS TO YOU?

Although poems can be about almost anything, the best poems are about things that matter to you. To begin finding a subject for your poem, take an inventory.

List ten things that interest you. Don't put down what you used to be interested in or what you think you ought to be interested in. Write down what you really care about, right now. Do not limit yourself to what you think is a suitable or passable subject for a poem.

Most likely, your list will include some abiding interests: football or figure skating, computers or chess. It can also include things that are close by as you create the list: your tropical fish, your stamp collection, the tapes or compact discs you've accumulated, your comic book collection, the view out your window, items of clothing, a vase of flowers, or a piece of fruit. Your inventory might even include some larger topics, such as the nature of evil or love.

Next, select three items from your list of ten: the one that you think will be easiest to write about, the one that would be hardest to write about, and the one that you think would make the best poem. Write each of these subjects in the middle of a large sheet of paper and then take some time—perhaps twenty minutes to an hour—to doodle and daydream about each one. Cover at least one sheet of paper with ideas, textures, feelings, insights, and items you associate with your topic. Just let yourself go. Don't ask yourself: "Why does an orange make me think of pain?" Just write down whatever comes to you somewhere on the sheet of paper that contains your topic.

Some people find it helpful to listen to music while brainstorming about their topics, and that may work for you. Don't watch television, though, because you want to keep your mind's eye—your imagination—free to "see" any images that appear to you. Make sure you write them all down.

Put these three pieces of paper away in a safe place—a folder or a large envelope—on a shelf or in a drawer. Ignore the pages for a little while, as you continue looking at and reading poems by other people. After some time has elapsed—overnight or up to three days—look at your pages again.

Are there words or phrases that seem powerful, moving, or important to you? Circle them and see if

*Your closest surroundings, such as a
child's wonder, can provide you with
numerous subjects for your writing.*

you can find any link among them. Sometimes you will find that you have written things that connect with other things on different pieces of paper, under different topics. Perhaps two or three of your topics are related.

Does anything leap out at you, announcing itself as a possible subject? Don't be surprised if you discover an entirely new and different topic for a poem, one that really excites you, among your scribbling. But whatever you decide to go with, make sure it matters to you.

LOOKING AT NATURE

In his *Letters to a Young Poet*, Ranier Maria Rilke advised a budding writer to get close to nature, in order to say "what you see and experience and love and lose." Looking into nature can provide excellent subject matter for poems. A walk in the woods, or the garden, a walk in a park, along a river, or the seashore, a hike in the mountains—even your walk to school—might give you ideas about subjects for poems. Just keep your eyes open and, if you can, jot down any thought you have as you walk.

There are always possibilities. You could write a poem on dandelions you see poking up between cracks in the sidewalk or about the different kinds of front yards you pass. Walt Whitman wrote an entire book called *Leaves of Grass*. There are numerous poems that use a single flower or tree as their subjects.

CITIES

You might consider writing a poem about a city. Whitman's poems of New York and Carl Sandburg's poems about Chicago serve as possible models. Grace Schulman has written wonderful contemporary

Cities have inspired poets for centuries. Carl Sandburg composed several poems about Chicago.

poems about New York, and Elizabeth Bishop wrote several fine poems about Paris.

Again, make sure the place has meaning to you and that you can provide details, no matter how gritty. You might include such details as the signs you see on buildings, the names of the newspapers displayed at a newsstand, or the language you hear being spoken around you.

ANIMALS

Animals make good subjects for poems, too. D. H. Lawrence wrote many poems about animals, as did Ted Hughes and Marianne Moore. Just make sure your animal is one you know well or can study in detail. It may even be an imaginary animal, such as a manticore or griffin.

Deciding to write a poem about a Bengal tiger when you've never seen one and haven't a chance of getting to a zoo may be setting yourself a very difficult task. Unless, of course, you write about your *longing* to see a Bengal tiger. Nothing is really out of the question.

HUMAN SUBJECTS

People make excellent subjects for poems. You could do a character sketch or a portrait of a person in words and turn that into a poem. Again, it's best to choose someone you know, someone about whom you have strong feelings—positive or negative. Some students enjoy writing about their grandparents, their siblings, or their best friends.

You could also write a poem that's a self-portrait— a picture of yourself. It might help you to look through some art books or to visit a local museum and study self-portraits by well-known painters. These can spark ideas about how to portray yourself. You might study a photograph of yourself and describe it or contemplate your reflection in a mirror and jot down what you see.

WRITING ABOUT PLACES

In his book *The Poetics of Space*, French philosopher Gaston Bachelard writes eloquently about the spaces we live in, and how we fill them with meaning through daydreams. He says:

> *Our house is our corner of the world. As has often been said, it is our first universe, a real cosmos in every sense of the word.... The house shelters daydreaming, the house protects the dreamer, the house allows one to dream in peace.*

Why not write a poem about a space in which you are safe and allowed to dream? Choose a significant spot: your grandmother's attic, a quiet area in a city park, a tree house by the pond. You might describe the most painful place you've ever been (the doctor's office? the principal's office?), the most mysterious place, or the place you go when you want to share a secret.

Whatever you choose, describe it all in great detail: the door's color, material, and weight; what the doorknob looks like; what covers the floor or what the floor is made of; how light enters the space and what it touches. What things are in the place you've chosen, and how did they get there?

GIVING ADVICE

Nazim Hikmet's poem "Advice to Those Who Would Spend Time in Prison" and Philip Booth's poem, "First

Lesson" both offer advice to cover specific situations that broaden in meaning and tell us how to live our lives. Is there something about which you feel confident giving advice—how to care for an animal, for example, or how to choose a hat? Consider that these might be doors into interesting poems.

The literal advice you give must be correct, so that anyone could follow it and accomplish the ostensible point of the poem. The trick is to broaden your advice so that it is meaningful on levels other than the merely literal.

MEMORIES

Memories, of course, are the stuff of poems, as they are the essence of snapshots. What we remember is what we love and what we are, and that's certainly worth writing about.

Many people remember their early childhood most vividly. What happens to us in our early years happens intensely. Like the first brilliant strokes of color on the white canvas, these events stand out clearly, usually for the rest of our lives. "Everybody writes about childhood," Elizabeth Bishop said. "You can't help it...you are fearfully observant then."

THE HIDDEN SUBJECT

If you can't come up with some nice crisp subject—some topic or area that is neatly delimited—don't give up. Some poets—John Ashbery, for instance—claim not to have subjects in mind when they sit down to write. Writing is an act of exploration rather than the following of a plan.

Of course, you can sit down at the page and just begin to explore. Play with words and images that interest you. Experiment with the music of words and see what happens. Let your subject emerge as your focus on it begins to clarify.

Be aware that most poems have more than one subject. There will be the overt, obvious subject, the one that triggered the writing of the poem: a groundhog, a hyacinth in bloom, or an encounter with a friend in the hall. Underneath will be another subject, one that you will probably discover in the process of writing your poem.

Hidden subjects tend to be larger than the original topic of the poem. But what are these hidden subjects that poetry addresses? Elizabeth Bishop put it this way: "Even before they've been lived through, a child can sense the great human subjects: time, which breeds loss, desire, the world's beauty."

Because these kinds of subjects will reveal themselves to you as you compose your poem, you don't have to worry about working them in. Just pick a topic, or a group of words, or an area of thought you feel you can write about—something that stirs your emotions and brings words to mind. Then put those words on paper.

FOUR

FIRST DRAFTS

Any time is the time to make a poem.
—Gertrude Stein

There is no secret to writing a poem. Just sit down and write one. Think about your subject and begin to put words on paper, one after another.

You can think about the shape that you want your poem to be and write in lines of a predetermined length. Or just let your language loose on the page, getting your words and ideas down rapidly, promising yourself you'll go back and clean it all up later.

Listen closely for the sound of the poem. Make sure you can hear what you want to say and transcribe it, writing it down instead of making it up.

Put down on paper the detailed, specific truth of your experience. Attend carefully to what you are saying. Say what you mean—don't just hunt around for feelings that fit the new words you've found in a thesaurus.

In your first draft, spare the reader nothing. Write down as much as possible. Don't save anything for later in the poem, or for another poem or another writing session. Write as if your life depended on it. Put all your energy and focus into the emergency of writing this poem, right now.

COMPOSING ON THE MOVE

Maybe you work better away from a piece of paper. Some poets have composed long pieces while driving for six or seven hours in their cars. Others like to compose on the bus, during a train ride, or while flying. Still other poets compose in their heads while walking. In fact, for some, poetry and walking are so closely connected that they wear out many pairs of shoes while working on their verses.

According to his widow, the Russian poet Osip Mandelstam usually paced the room or went outside to walk the streets when he was composing a poem. She writes that the process of composing verse involves:

> *the recollection of something that has never before been said, and the search for lost words is an attempt to remember what is still to be brought into being.... This requires great concentration, till whatever has been forgotten flashes suddenly into the mind...the recollection is developed like the image on a photographic plate.*

IF YOU CAN'T JUST WRITE

Perhaps you want—or need—more detailed directions for creating your poem. Some tips and techniques to get you started follow, but remember: every poem is different and wants to be written its own way, in its own time. What works for others may work for you, but it may not.

No matter how crazy it seems, whatever is most comfortable for you is the right way to compose a poem. If you find that you write well after everyone in the house has gone to sleep, with the covers pulled up over your head, and your work illuminated by flashlight, then that is the way you should write.

PREPARING THE GROUND

One foolproof way to get started is to work with the freewriting exercise described in the previous chapter. You will find, if you write freely for a few days, that certain topics and phrases obsess you. They appear again and again as you write. You may not even need to read what you've written in order to know these words. They're the ones you always use to begin when you don't know what you want to say.

Try using these words to start a poem. For instance, let's say you always begin writing by putting down that old typing exercise, "The quick brown fox jumped over the lazy dog." How can you use that tired sentence to begin?

You might start by seeing the fox in your mind's eye and describing it. Maybe she's more reddish than brown and is darting across a country road at night, leaving you only the impression of red speed and the flash of her white-tipped tail as she disappears into the bushes. For inspiration on how this kind of vision might become a poem, look at Ted Hughes's poem "The Thought Fox."

Maybe that lazy dog really interests you. See the lazy dog in your imagination. Remember that stuffed dog you used to have, and how it just laid on your bed for days and weeks and years, until it finally was lost in a move or disappeared. Now you are into a memory of something that matters to you, and you can begin to write your poem.

WRITING REQUIRES PATIENCE

If, as you sit down to write your poem, you find yourself staring at paper, wanting to write and not quite feeling up to it, please do not despair. Writing poetry isn't something that can be willed, as, say, you can will yourself to write a check or a list of things to buy at the supermarket.

Your imagination won't be ordered around, and good thoughts tend to come slowly and quietly. Inspiration rarely arrives in a lightning flash. More often, it announces itself somewhat mildly, clearing its throat, say, or dropping a handkerchief, or beginning as a kind of hum inside your head.

Writing a poem will take time, and some of that time will be spent idly doodling, staring into space, pacing, perhaps even biting your nails. That's just the way it is.

Even great and famous writers experience difficulty in getting words down on paper. As Pulitzer Prize–winning poet Louise Glück wrote:

> *The fundamental experience of the writer is helplessness...most writers spend most of their time in various kinds of torment: wanting to write, being unable to write; wanting to write differently, being unable to write differently. In a whole lifetime, years are spent waiting to be claimed by an idea.*

LOWERING YOUR STANDARDS

While this is true, it is not the whole truth. In spite of the difficulty of beginning work, people do write poems. Getting started can merely be a matter of lowering your standards. Or, as a friend once said, "Anything worth doing is worth doing badly." So

Pulitzer Prize–winning poet Louise Glück

decide that you will write a poem—not a good poem, or a great poem, or even a passable poem. You will write a poem. Period. Then write it.

It may help to remember that the beginning of anything is usually slow going. Recognize that getting started could take a while, and don't give up before you've really given yourself a chance.

OPENINGS

For some writers, openings, or beginnings, are easy. Even Elizabeth Bishop, who composed slowly and painfully, admitted that starting a poem was simple. "I begin lots of things and then I give up on them," she said.

Sometimes first lines are givens: they appear in one's head with little or no prompting. Other times, writing the first line of a poem can be very difficult, but once you get it, something in the tone or the rhythm or the syntax tells you just what to write next.

Many poets do not find their first lines until somewhat later in the process of writing. Only in later drafts, well into the process of revision, does the true first line of the poem emerge.

Obviously, you must find a method that works for you. There is no law that says you must begin a poem at the beginning, although that generally is the case. Or, as W. H. Auden said: "Usually, of course, one starts at the beginning and works through to the end. Sometimes, though, one starts with a certain line in mind, perhaps a last line."

And even if you do start at the beginning—well, everything changes in the course of writing a successful poem. Auden again: "One starts, I think, with a certain idea of thematic organization, but this usually alters during the process of writing."

THE NATURE OF FIRST LINES

The first line of a poem is an invitation. It can be engraved on heavy white vellum or scrawled on a preprinted card; it can be a telephone call or a yell across the school yard: "Come over Saturday!"

There are as many good ways to open a poem as there are to issue an invitation. Just remember, the point is to get the reader interested in what you have to say and willing to read more.

Here are some ideas for ways to create an interesting first line:

- With a question:
  Shall I compare thee to a summer's day?
  (William Shakespeare, Sonnet XVIII)

- With a comparison:
  My love is like a red, red rose
  (Robert Burns, "My Love Is...")

- With an address to the subject (apostrophe):
  Tyger! Tyger! burning bright
  (William Blake, "The Tyger")
  Milton, wouldst thou were living at this hour
  (William Wordsworth, "To Milton")
  Season of mists and mellow fruitfulness
  (John Keats, "Ode to Autumn")

- With the beginning of a story:
  I caught a tremendous fish
  (Elizabeth Bishop, "The Fish")

- In the middle of a story:
  While spoon-feeding him with one hand
  she holds his hand with her other hand.
  (Galway Kinnell, "Parkinson's Disease")

- With an observation:
  Clearly, the lake is too large.
  (Margaret Ryan, "Lac D'Amour")

- With a counterfactual condition:
  Had we but world enough and time
  (Andrew Marvell, "To His Coy Mistress")
  If I had not met the red haired boy whose father
  (W. S. Merwin, "One of the Lives")

These are only a few suggestions. In general, while you want your opening to be attractive, beckoning, provocative, you don't want it to be the high point of your poem. Poems usually build from the opening, so it's okay for your beginning to be a little low-key; just make sure it isn't boring.

Look at some poems you like and try to discover additional ways to invite the reader in. Freshness, allure, and authority make a first line appealing and will help to make the reader curious about what comes next.

Most good openings are musically appealing— they have a certain ring to them. Bad openings, on the other hand, turn the reader away, or at least put the reader off. Longfellow's opening for the poem *The Song of Hiawatha*, for instance, is to many readers less than inviting: "By the shores of Gitche Gumee."

MIDDLES

Narrative line is a vitally important element of poetry that is not often mentioned. Yet even the most imaginative poems have some basis in fact or common sense. And because we live in time, most readers expect poems to have a beginning, a middle, and an end that follow in a kind of natural sequence.

Once you have begun, you must tell the reader the rest of the story—the rest of the feeling—in a way that is possible to follow. Make sure your action, even if it's just the emotional action of the poem, unfolds logically. Let it unfold seamlessly as a dream, rather than skipping around all over the place. If there is a seed in the poem, have it sprout, grow leaves, and bud *before* it blossoms.

Of course, you don't have to put all these steps into the poem; just don't have them occur in the wrong order, or you will lose your reader. You want to lead the reader from line to line logically and emotionally all at once. This doesn't mean you have to include every detail. You want the ones that really count.

Take a look at the ballad "Sir Patrick Spens," for example, which begins this way:

> *The king sits in Dumferling town,*
> *Drinking the bluide-red wine:*
> *"O whar will I get guid sailor,*
> *To sail this schip of mine?"*
>
> *Up and spak an eltern knicht.*
> *Sat at the king's richt kne:*
> *"Sir Patrick Spense is the best sailor*
> *That sails upon the sea."*
>
> *The king has written a braid letter,*
> *And signed it with his hand:*
> *And sent it to Sir Patrick Spens,*
> *Was walking on the sand.*

The poem continues for several more verses and, as poet Richard Moore points out in his essay "Seven Types of Accuracy," tells:

> *a condensed and laconic story that moves rather abruptly from vivid detail to vivid detail. New stanzas plunge us without warning into new scenes. It is as accurate as a fine definition in mathematics—and as inspired.*

As you write your first draft, try to get everything that belongs in the middle of the poem into a logical order. Keep the action moving forward. Make sure that every line you add advances the reader's knowledge of the situation, the feeling, or the action you're trying to convey.

ENDINGS

When an interviewer asked how long it took to finish her poem "The Moose," Elizabeth Bishop answered: "I started that years ago—twenty years at least—I had a stack of notes—the first two or three stanzas—and the last."

Having the ending doesn't necessarily mean a poem is finished. But a poem can't be finished without an ending. You want a final line—or stanza—to resolve whatever conflict has occurred in the poem. At the same time, you want the ending to reverberate, to ring in the air beyond the poem.

There are many ways to end a poem. Here are a few:

- With an image:
  The thin hound's body arched against
      the snow.
          (Louise Bogan, "Old Countryside")
  Uneasy, treacherous green water.
          (Amy Clampitt, "The Matrix")

- With a statement:
  As like as not, when they take life over their
      door-sills
  They should let it go by.
          (Louise Bogan, "Women")
  The mind gropes toward its own recessional.
          (Amy Clampitt, "Manhatten-Staten
              Island Ferry")

- With a question:
  How can we know the dancer from
      the dance?
          (W. B. Yeats, "Among School Children")
  Fled is that music. Do I wake or sleep?
          (John Keats, "Ode to a Nightingale")

Who fell. For what? Can someone tell us?
  (Amy Clampitt, "War Memorial")

- With a predicament:
  It's hard to know which life is sleep,
  Or where the door is with my real name on it.
    (Robert Winner, "The Banjo")

- With a string of fragmented words:
  Ecstasy, hunger.
    (Brendan Kennelly, "The Teachers")

- With the lilt of a song:
  Because what is is good.
    (Brendan Kennelly, "So")

- With a bit of everyday speech:
  No stranger, finally, to the mystery of what
      we are.
    (Amy Clampitt, "Matoaka")

- With an unconscious flash:
  That the river is nobody's friend.
    (Brendan Kennelly, "The Shannon")

- With a new possibility:
  O remember
  In your narrowing dark tower
  That more things move
  Than blood in the heart.
    (Louise Bogan, "Night")

- By circling back to earlier material. Thulani
  Davis's poem "boppin' is safer than grindin'"
  begins:
  I danced on "Shop Around"
  but never on the flip side
  "Who's Lovin' You"
  boppin' was safer than grindin'
      (which is why you should not
          come around)

The poem ends this way:

...let's make a pact
not to bruise each other
or kiss each other with all we've got
cause boppin' is safer than grindin'
& I'd rather dance to "Shop Around"
than "Who's Lovin' You"

- With a comparison:
    The shadows stoop over like guests at
        a christening.
            (Sylvia Plath, "Candles")
    The clear vowels rise like balloons.
        (Sylvia Plath, "Morning Song")

THE SOUND OF AN ENDING

As with the opening line of a poem, the final line should be musical. It should also sound final. Sometimes it's helpful to tie up the ending of a poem by using rhyme, even if the poem has not rhymed throughout. The rhyming of final lines can provide a sense of closure, giving the reader a feeling of finality, and satisfaction.

Everything was rainbow, rainbow, rainbow
And I let the fish go.
    (Elizabeth Bishop, "The Fish")

GETTING READY FOR REVISION

Once you have written your draft all the way through, take a break. Let some time elapse. When you look at the poem again, it should look fresh to you, almost as if someone else wrote it. Then you know it is time for rewriting, or revision.

FIVE

GETTING SPECIFIC

Go in fear of abstractions.
—Ezra Pound

Once you have a draft of your poem, read through it slowly and critically. Underline or circle all the abstract words. They are the words that name ideas, concepts, things we cannot touch. Courage, hope, prosperity, ambition, faith, and fear are all abstractions.

Then, using a different-colored pen or pencil, underline or circle all the concrete, specific details in your draft. If you've mentioned that the boy you liked in second grade had curly red hair, that is specific. If you've named the river you're describing—the Colorado, the Hudson, the Mississippi, the Congo, the Amazon—that is also specific. If you've drawn, in words, a three-story brick house or a dandelion that's just gone to seed, that is specific. Underline those things.

Don't be surprised if you have found more abstract words in the first draft of your poem than concrete ones. Beginning poets tend to work in abstractions, and with good reason. Many of the things that inspire poetry—love and hate, war and peace, life and death—are most comfortably dealt with in the abstract. That way, the writer can generalize and distance these big issues from his or her physical self. It is much easier to write about death in general than to write about the specific death of a beloved pet.

Then, too, abstractions sometimes sound more important than concrete and specific details. But although they sound impressive, abstractions can be hard to understand because there is nothing for the senses to grasp.

POETRY IS IN THE DETAILS

"It's the knack for noticing specific things that enlarges our awareness of the world," Julia Cameron writes in *The Artist's Way*. And it's the specific, concrete details that give life and texture to poetry and convey your awareness of the world to others.

That's why beginning writers are often advised: "Show, don't tell." Readers want to see for themselves and draw their own conclusions. If you say "a well-dressed woman," you are *telling*. If you describe her hat and gloves, the color and cut of her clothes, the arch of her eyebrows, her carefully made-up eyes in such a way as to suggest a well-dressed woman, you are *showing*. Your readers are led to generalize (a well-dressed woman) from the specific details you have chosen and presented.

You will find, as you read and write poetry, that the best way to communicate your ideas about large, general subjects is to use the most particular details. Grasping this paradox can be the first, and potentially the most difficult, step on the road to writing poetry. Getting past this paradox, on the other hand, and beginning to write poems that are rooted in the real, filled with detail and sense words, generally creates an immediate and amazing improvement in the quality of a writer's poetry.

ABSTRACT vs. CONCRETE

An image, according to John Frederick Nims in his classic book about poetry, *Western Wind*, is "a piece of news from the world outside or from our own bodies which is brought into the light of consciousness through one of the senses."

Images are different from ideas and words because images are full of sensory information. Color, taste, texture, sound, and scent are the stuff of images. As you would expect, images are generally concrete: roses, rain, and steel are all concrete images. Ideas, on the other hand, are abstract: horticulture, meteorology, and metallurgy are all abstract.

Most people agree that it's easier and more effective to communicate in poems through sense detail and concrete images. But there are those who appear to disagree. American poet Wallace Stevens, for example, wrote a poem entitled "The Ultimate Poem Is Abstract." And in his poem "Notes Toward a Supreme Fiction," Stevens called the first section, "It must be abstract."

Even abstractions need some physical details if they are going to be communicated effectively. When Wallace Stevens writes about abstraction in "Notes Toward a Supreme Fiction," he uses images of the sun, the eye, "a voluminous master folded in his fire." In order to talk about *abstract ideas*, Stevens uses *concrete things*.

American poet William Carlos Williams, however, wrote, "No ideas but in things." Perhaps you know his poem about the red wheelbarrow; it is a very concrete poem with a strong visual image.

A PLACE FOR ABSTRACTION?

Obviously, there are at least two schools of thought on the subject of abstraction and its role in poetry. You will have to decide whether you prefer your poems filled with words that name things, making them easier for your reader to "see" in his or her imagination, or whether you prefer to work in abstract terms.

Keep in mind that concrete, specific language makes it easier to communicate with your reader. This is not to say that there is no place for abstractions in poetry; rather, keep in mind the *ratio* of concrete images to abstractions in your work. Let concrete, specific language predominate. Then your readers will be able to grasp the remaining abstractions more easily.

Amy Clampitt's poem, "The Smaller Orchid," for example, begins with an abstraction; yet the complete poem is composed largely of quite specific, concrete details:

THE SMALLER ORCHID

Love is a climate
small things find safe
to grow in—not
(though I once supposed so)
the demanding cattleya
du cote de chez Swann,
glamour among the faubourgs,
hothouse overpowerings, blisses
and cruelties at teatime, but this
next-to-unidentifiable wildling,
hardly more than a
sprout, I've found
flourishing in the hollows
of a granite seashore—

a cheerful tousle, little,
white, down-to-earth orchid
declaring its authenticity,
if you hug the ground
close enough, in a powerful
outdoorsy-domestic
whiff of vanilla.

Ideas, such as life, death, and love, are both abstract and concrete. These exist as concepts and as embodied realities. The *idea* of a tree and *real* trees both exist.

It's the nature of poetry to deal with the concrete embodiments of abstractions and the particular instances of generalities. But because we are sensory creatures, it is best to clothe your ideas in flesh and blood and bone. By all means, write a poem about love but let it portray a particular instance of loving, the love of a mother for a child, a child for a parent, a particular woman for a particular man. Let the reader generalize about love in the abstract from the specific instance you present.

IMAGES

Images are everywhere. The poet's work is to catch them. Perhaps they occur to you naturally. You perceive the falling leaves as great yellow carp swimming in the pool of a blue October sky. When you hear a horn blaring, it sears your ears like fire, or you have a sudden sensation of brass.

If making concrete, sensory images doesn't come naturally to you, here are some suggestions that might help:

- Read Imagist poets. H. D. (Hilda Doolittle) is one you might enjoy.

- Sit in a public space, a place where people pass. You might try a coffee shop, a train station, a park bench, or a busy library. Observe what happens around you. Describe it in writing. Take notes. When you read through your notes later, see how many specifics you have captured, how many details that appeal to the senses. Can you use the notes you've made to write a draft of a poem?
- Reconstruct a memory. Put yourself back in a favorite place and imagine every detail. What did the ceiling in your childhood bedroom look like? Was it painted or papered? Was there a light fixture? Was it plaster or gypsum board? Was it smooth or bumpy?
- Study a photo or a painting. Note the details in words.

APPEALING TO THE SENSES

Appealing to the senses is a reliable way to engage the imaginations of your readers. William Blake called the senses "the chief inlets of the soul." And W. H. Auden said that "the wildest poem has to have a firm basis in common sense." Common sense is what we all know because our five senses tell us about the world in which we live. If you have doubts about the relationship of the senses to the imagination, try this experiment.

Think about a lemon, a particular lemon. Imagine its waxy fragrant rind, its bright yellow shine, the sharp citrus scent. Imagine the weight of the lemon in your hand. You are lifting it slowly to your lips. You take a bite. Your teeth sink through the rind, right into the pale yellow flesh of the lemon.

Did your salivary glands respond by producing a spurt of saliva within your mouth? If you merely think about the words *tart* or *bitter* do you get the same reaction?

Sensory specifics definitely help to get the reader's imagination in gear. So if you want your readers to experience what you want to communicate, make sure your writing appeals to the senses.

Look over your draft and see if there's any opportunity for you to put sense words to use—words that allow the reader to see, hear, smell, touch, and taste what you are talking about.

Through sensory details, a poem communicates the poet's ideas and feelings about what it means to be mortal, to love, or to loathe.

SEEING

Sight is important in poetry. Often, poets use visual language to help readers "see" what they are describing.

The Imagist movement in the early part of this century put an emphasis on using language to create pictures. Many poems are written about works of visual art, including sculpture, paintings, and photographs.

Some poets go to visual extremes and write poems in the shapes of pictures. John Hollander and George Herbert are two poets whose poems are arranged on the page to look like objects: a bottle, a butterfly.

But even if you are not drawing pictures with poems, the shape of the words on the page has a visual effect on readers. The way lines move and turn, the size of stanzas, whether lines are indented or are flush with the left margins, create different expectations within your readers.

Poets often look beyond the surface of things, trying to understand the object's true meaning. To convey that meaning to the reader, the poet needs to present the same visual data as they, themselves, are reacting to. This makes it easier for the reader to share in the poet's experience. In Amy Clampitt's poem about the orchid, for example, we are by the poem's end enabled to see what the poet is seeing. And in William Wordsworth's sonnet "I Wandered Lonely as a Cloud," we are given the poet's vision of daffodils:

> *When all at once I saw a crowd,*
> *A host, of golden daffodils;*
> *Beside the lake, beneath the trees,*
> *Fluttering and dancing in the breeze.*

HEARING

Many words sound like what they mean. Buzz, for example, sounds like the noise that bees, flies, and chain saws make. Words that sound like what they mean are called onomatopoeic words. There are many such words in English: *crash, bang, boom*. They convey information that appeals to the sense of hearing.

Combinations of words can also recreate sounds: *The humming of innumerable bees*, for example, creates the sound it describes. The poetry of John Keats is full of sensual imagery. Listen to the music of these lines:

> *The music, yearning like a God in pain*

> *The key turns, and the door upon its hinges*
>   *groans.*
> > ("Eve of Saint Agnes")

> *The murmurous haunt of flies on summer eves.*
> > ("Ode to a Nightingale")

See chapter ten, "The Music of Poetry," for a more extended discussion of sound.

*John Keats, shown here in his study,
wrote poetry characterized by sensual imagery
and skillful manipulation of sound.*

TASTE

Proust's famous novel *Remembrance of Things Past* unwinds from an experience of taste. A madeleine, a shell-shaped teacake, dipped into linden flower tea erupts into memories on the author's tongue. It is a clear lesson in the power of taste to recall lost worlds.

Words such as *bitter*, *tart*, and *sweet* are taste words. You can also suggest tastes just by naming things we eat:

> *She found me roots of relish sweet,*
> *And honey wild, and manna dew....*
>   (John Keats, "La Belle Dame sans Merci")

You can also use comparisons to introduce the element of taste into your poems. "Her lips were ripe Bing cherries" conveys both a visual image (the red-black color, roundness), and at the same time, a taste image (the sweetness of ripe fruit). Mixing sensory images is called *synesthesia*. In the Clampitt poem, "The Smaller Orchid," quoted above, for example, the "whiff of vanilla" is an image of both taste and smell.

SMELL

Scents are evocative; a single whiff of a certain perfume can bring back vivid memories. The scent of rain, or carnations, or baking bread can recreate worlds for you, and for your readers. What does the foliage of a tomato plant smell like? What do heaps of fallen leaves smell like in autumn? How would you describe the scent of the sea?

It's possible to introduce scent into a poem merely by comparing something you see to something that smells fragrant.

Keats does this when he compares the clouds of an old man's breath on a cold night to "pious incense from a censor old" in his poem, "The Eve of St Agnes."

Of course, you could also use an extended passage to bring perfumes to an imaginative life. In "Ode to a Nightingale," for instance, Keats's speaker stands in the dark, taking in the perfume of the night:

I cannot see what flowers are at my feet,
Nor what soft incense hangs upon the bough,
But in embalmed darkness, guess each sweet
Wherewith the seasonable month endows
The grass, the thicket, and the fruit tree wild…

TOUCH

The smoothness of silk, the rough texture of bark; these are images that appeal to the sense of touch. Expressions such as "the soft sea-sand," (Landor), "the downy owl" (Keats), "rough ashes" (Keats), and "ribbed and torchlike" (D. H. Lawrence) appeal to both the sense of touch and the eye. While they tell you the way things look, they also tell you the way they feel. Are there places in your draft where you could convey additional information about the look and texture of something you mentioned?

WORKING FROM ABSTRACTIONS

Let us suppose that you have uncovered a number of abstractions in the first draft of your poem. How can you make some of those abstractions concrete?

The best way to describe your feelings is not to tell the reader how you feel: tired, scared, etc., but to tell what you saw, smelled, tasted, touched and heard.

Consider, for instance, this statement from the first draft of a poem: "The fire scared me." While the words state a fact, they don't help the reader feel the poet's fear. Both *fire* and *scare* are distancing; they remove the reader from both the heat and the fear. But both ideas can be made physically vivid for the reader:

I saw red flames leap near the windows,
a red glow spread across the sky.
The air—thick, black, pungent—
smelled of burning wood.
I leaned against the wall.
Heat seared my shirt.
In the distance, the scream of fire engines.
Their clanking bells growing nearer.

As you can see, adding sensory details will often make your draft longer. That's because you will be expanding any shorthand you've used in your poem by translating the telegraphic, intellectual statements into physical details that are easy for your reader to feel and share.

SITING THE POEM

Everything happens in a particular place and time. It helps your reader greatly to know just where he or she is as the poem begins.

Robert Frost is a master of setting poems in place and time. Sometimes he does it in a title: "Stopping by Woods on a Snowy Evening" tells you where and when the poem is taking place. In other poems, Frost establishes the place and time in the opening lines: "Two roads diverged in a yellow wood" certainly lets the reader know just where he or she stands—and what the season is—as the poem begins.

Not every poem needs to be anchored in real space and real time, but most should be. Review your draft again. Have you positioned your poem in space and time for your reader? Is it taking place in a setting that the reader can see, or at least imagine?

Try introducing the elements of place and time early in your draft. Is it dawn or dusk? Morning or evening? Summer or winter? Is the poem taking place a hundred years ago or yesterday? You don't have to state these facts baldly. Think about how you can indicate them with a word, a phrase, a specific detail. You might, for example, begin by describing the landscape:

> *On either side of the river lie*
> *Long fields of barley and of rye.*
> (Alfred, Lord Tennyson, "The Lady of Shallot")

Or simply state who and where the characters in the poem are:

> *My grandfather said to me*
> *as we sat on the wagon seat*
> (Elizabeth Bishop, "Manners")

If you cannot work the details of time and space into your opening lines, or for some reason don't want to, consider selecting a title for your poem that allows the reader to place themselves in space and time. Why not look at the table of contents of poetry anthologies and see if you can find titles that immediately place the poem in space and/or time. Among the works of Elizabeth Bishop, for example, you will find titles such as "Paris, 7 A.M." and "Crusoe in England."

NAMING

Being specific can include calling objects by name. *Flower* is not an abstraction, but it is not specific. Is it a rose or a tulip? A dandelion or a pansy? Is it *phlox divericata*, White Admiral, or Dodo Hanbury Forbes? If you don't know the real specific names of some of the things in your poem, why not do some research?

It's vital for writers to know the names of things, and especially for beginning poets to know the names of the plants and animals that live in their neighborhood or part of the country. Learning these names can be fun, a kind of detective work.

Look for names in visual dictionaries or in the encyclopedia. Sign up for weed walks or garden tours. Visit the zoo, the pet shop, or nature preserves. Read nature guides to shells, birds, trees, and flowers, and learn their names. That way, you'll be able to get specific when you need to. Do you want to write about your pet, your dog, your golden retriever, or Rover? Naming precisely can make a difference.

HINTS FOR REVISION

- Reread your draft.
- Are there places where you can turn abstractions into concretions?
- Can you add sense words?
- Is the poem set in time and place? If not, how can you do that?
- Can you name something in your poem more specifically in order to help your reader see it more clearly?

Make any changes that you feel will improve your original draft.

SIX

FIGURES OF SPEECH

*The metaphor is probably the most fertile power
possessed by man [or woman!]*
—José Ortega y Gasset

Using figures of speech, or figurative language, can help to make your poem more concrete while you deepen the meaning beyond the merely literal. Perhaps you've already used some figures of speech. If you've made comparisons ("My love is like a red, red rose") or personified some inanimate object ("O rose, thou art sick") you have used figurative language naturally. In this chapter, you will learn how to recognize and use figures of speech, how to add them to your poem, and how to strengthen those you've used already.

FIGURATIVE vs. LITERAL

Poet Robert Frost once noted that poetry is "the one permissible way of saying one thing and meaning another." Poetry is able to do this through figurative language, because such language points beyond the explicit meaning of words to suggest another, perhaps deeper, meaning.

It may sound like an odd and unfamiliar way to use language, but, in fact, it's common practice. When you're driving along the highway, for instance, and see a sign that says, "Rough Road Ahead," chances are the sign literally means what it says. You can expect the paved surface to be bumpy up ahead. This is using language to say what actually *is*.

But suppose you run into an old friend and ask, "How's your exam schedule?" and your friend replies, "Rough road ahead." You probably do not think your friend is talking about the state of the pavement over which he or she is about to travel. Instead, you know that your friend is saying that things are tough, that he or she expects the going to be hard, and that it isn't all going to be smooth sailing.

Your friend is using language figuratively, and you are easily translating the meaning. You understand the connotation of the words—the secondary meaning your friend is trying to suggest beyond the literal, or surface level, of the words.

Figures of speech are a way to make writing more colorful and more specific. They also provide sensory information. In the figure of the "rough road," for example, we immediately understand something of how life feels for someone else.

Use figures of speech in your poem to convey the feelings you want to share. First, consider some of the most commonly used figures of speech. Then, consider how to introduce them into the draft of your poem.

COMPARISONS

Comparison is the most basic figure of speech. We use comparisons all the time. When we ask someone for information—about an event we didn't attend, a place we've never visited, a meeting with an extraordinary person, we ask, "What was it like? What was she like?"

We learn by equating the unknown with the known. Describing a stranger, for example, we might say she has hair like Aunt Anne, a nose like our friend Julius, and she dresses just like Barbara Bush.

Poetry generally uses two kinds of comparisons: similes and metaphors.

SIMILES

Similes are comparisons that use the words *like* or *as*. Similes occur frequently in everyday speech. Whenever we say: *sober as a judge, drunk as a sailor, white as snow, dark as night*, or *fierce as a tiger*, we are using a simile.

The folk song "Sometimes I Feel Like a Motherless Child" is built entirely of similes, and through repetition they gain great power. If you've never heard the song, ask your librarian to help you find a recording of Paul Robeson performing it. The song includes the following lines:

> *Sometimes I feel like a motherless child.*
> *Sometimes I feel like I have no friend.*
> *Sometimes I feel like a feather in air.*
> *Sometimes I feel like I'm almost gone.*

These are simple, yet powerful statements. They convey a great deal of information about how the speaker in fact feels. Is there a place in the draft of your poem where you try to state how you feel?

> *I feel sad.*
> *I felt miserable.*

If so, try using a comparison instead:

> *I feel like a weeping willow tree.*
> *I felt like a beggar soaked through with*
>   *cold rain.*

You could even write an entire poem based on simile, following the pattern of "Sometimes I Feel Like a Motherless Child." Begin each line with "Sometimes I feel..." and complete the lines by stating concrete specific things you feel like:

> *Sometimes I feel like a field full of weeds.*
> *Sometimes I feel like a red fire truck.*
> *Sometimes I feel like an atom bomb.*
> *Sometimes I feel like melted ice cream.*

If you'd like, you can extend each of these lines, adding a descriptive action phrase:

> *Sometimes I feel like a red fire truck speeding*
>   *down the block toward a false alarm.*
> *Sometimes I feel like melted ice cream*
>   *dribbling down a toddler's chin.*

Even one of these kinds of comparisons can get you started on a poem. Or you can use several of them to paint a more complex picture of how you feel.

METAPHORS

Metaphors are comparisons that do not use the words *like* or *as*. Instead, in a metaphor the comparison is implied. When we say that a particular project has been smooth sailing, for example, we are comparing the project to a voyage, even though we don't use *like* or *as*.

In general, similes are more easygoing and relaxed than metaphors. Similes say something is *like* something else, whereas metaphors say one thing is the *same* as another. Metaphors tend to be more powerful:

> *The evening was as quiet as a nun.*
> *The evening was a nun.*
> *My love is like a red, red rose.*
> *My love is a red red rose.*

Clearly, there are two different levels of meaning, one more forceful than the other.

HINTS ON MAKING COMPARISONS

Aristotle wrote that having command of metaphor—being able to make comparisons that are insightful, that tell us something new about the world and about ourselves—was the mark of genius in a poet. Perhaps the gift of seeing comparisons is a mark of genius, but the fact is, the rest of us mere mortals can also learn to handle simile and metaphor pretty well. It calls for attention and practice.

In the best comparisons, you are able to say that one thing is exactly like another. For example, in Elizabeth Bishop's poem "Crusoe in England":

> *The turtles lumbered by, high-domed,*
> *hissing like teakettles.*

To find good comparisons to use in similes and metaphors, be alert for the almost hidden links between things. As you ride the bus or wait in line, observe what's around you and see what it suggests to you. Ask yourself, "What is it like?"

USING COMPARISONS TO GET CONCRETE

One error that beginning writers often make in using comparison is to rely on it too heavily. When this occurs, the only concrete solid objects in the poem are those to which abstractions are compared:

- Guilt is the wet laundry room of hate.
- Accept the fire of pain into your life.
- Her soul is tender as a first-rate steak.

These are ridiculous lines, but part of their hilarity is the result of the metaphor or simile comparing abstractions (guilt, pain, soul) to concrete things (laundry room, fire, steak).

Comparisons work much better when you compare concrete objects to other concrete objects: turtles to teakettles, for example. That way, the reader can see, hear, feel, smell, taste, and touch the reality you are trying to present.

Look again at the draft of your poem. Choose an abstraction and compare it to something concrete.

Beauty is like...
Truth is like...
Absence is like...

Now see if you can substitute the concrete thing, the genuine article, for the abstraction in your poem. For instance, if you write "Absence is like a toothache," see if you can write a poem about a toothache that never mentions absence, yet conveys the feeling of absence to your reader. Or you might compile a list of all the things your abstraction is like and let that list become your poem, using the abstraction as a title:

COMFORT

Clean sheets. A book of poems. A cup of tea.
When it's wet outside, being warm and dry
under a down comforter. Steam banging up
through heating pipes. A slice of pumpkin pie.

Try taking something you have described sketchily, or less than fully, in your poem and compare it to something else.

My dog is like...
Her hat was like...
His hands were like...

See if this helps you to add detail and concreteness to your poem.

WHAT TO AVOID

There are many pitfalls in using comparisons, but three deserve special attention.

The first is known as a *mixed metaphor*, that is, a metaphor that combines terms from very different areas, is logically incorrect, and often humorous:

She had the kind of eye that could say...
The flood was a pestilence.
The trees were up to their ankles in mud
The soup of human kindness oozed from
the earth.
He was the designer who changed the face of
neck wear.

Mixed metaphors tend to be obvious—to everyone except their creator. It's always a good idea to have someone you trust—a friend, teacher, sibling, or parent—read through your work to spot errors of this sort.

Clichés are the second danger in using comparisons. You don't want to use either dead metaphors or comparisons that are so tired that they have slipped into the category of cliché. Cliché is language that has been so overused that it offers no fresh or surprising insight to the reader. *Sober as a judge, weary as the dead, black as night, quiet as a mouse*—these are similes that have become clichés.

Dead metaphors have been used so long that they have become part of the fabric of the language. In the previous sentence, *fabric* is a dead metaphor.

Look for fresh comparisons, ones that give the reader an exciting new view of both elements you are comparing:

> *Let this eye be an eagle,*
> *This lip the shadow of an abyss.*
> > (Sylvia Plath, "Gulliver")

> *The mind is an enchanting thing*
> * like the glaze on a*
> *katydid wing*
> * subdivided by sun*
> * till the nettings are legion.*
> > (Marianne Moore, "Mind")

Finally, don't overdo comparisons in a poem. Similes and metaphors can add some snap, but pile up too many and your reader will lose sight of what your poem is really about. As Dorothy Parker once wrote in reviewing a writer's first novel, "If he doesn't watch his pen, he might simile himself to death."

SYNECDOCHE AND METONYMY

Synecdoche and metonymy are figures of speech that are distant cousins of metaphor. *Synecdoche* means substituting a part for the whole, or vice versa. It may sound unusual, but we use synecdoche often in ordinary discourse. "All hands on deck" substitutes a part (hands) for the whole (sailors).

In *metonymy*, you replace the name of something with something closely related to it. "Who's the suit?" substitutes a piece of clothing for a person. When we say "Give us this day our daily bread," we are substituting *bread* for all kinds of food.

PERSONIFICATION

Personification attributes human feelings to inanimate or abstract objects.

"Hope, thou bold taster of delight." Keats, in his "Ode to Autumn," gives an abstraction, hope, the ability to taste, and what's more, to do so boldly.

Personification, or anthropomorphism, is an easy figure to use. Unfortunately, it's also easy to misuse. Be careful about ascribing human feelings and actions to inanimate objects. You may end up with an overly sentimental poem, or something so treacly sweet it makes your teeth hurt. Here's a bad example of personification:

> *The sky cried out to me,*
> *I love the earth below.*
> *The earth had turned her head.*
> *And it began to snow.*

Another pitfall to avoid is the *pathetic fallacy*—the idea that nature mirrors us and our feelings. When you have trees weeping, the wind moaning, or leaves whispering, make sure it's not too cute, sentimental, or maudlin. And if a tree must whisper in your poetry, or an animal speak, make sure it has something *really* interesting to say.

APOSTROPHE

Apostrophe—addressing something inanimate or abstract as if it were a person—is another sort of personification. It means addressing, or talking to, something that can't possibly be listening. This figure of speech was popular among poets of the romantic period. Keats spoke to nightingales and Grecian urns, Percy Bysshe Shelley called out to the western wind, and Wordsworth called out to Milton (already long dead), as well as to Duty.

Apostrophes now tend to sound dated. These days, the figure of speech might be used ironically or satirically. Like personification, apostrophe is easy to use, but very difficult to use well.

SYMBOLS

In poetry, things *are*. They also represent, or stand for, other unseen things. *Symbols* are images that resonate with meaning and recur throughout a poem. They have sometimes been described as metaphors with the first term omitted. The cross, for example, is a symbol; it stands for itself and for Christianity. A red rose can symbolize love.

Generally, symbols are images so loaded with meaning that they almost transcend the literal. They are themselves and, at the same time, a manifestation of something else that is too complicated or intangible to be revealed.

When looking for, making up, or using symbols, don't forget that things *are* before they *represent*. Before something can be a symbol, it must be real. As Richard Moore writes, "To see a line first as symbolic is to ignore almost all of its force as poetry."

ALLUSION

Allusions are references to literary works or other outside knowledge a reader is expected to know or at least recognize. Allusions are often classical; that is, referring to the cultures and myths of Greece or Rome. When a poem refers to Leda and the Swan, or Hercules, or Ulysses, the author is making a classical allusion.

Of course, not all allusions are classical. Writers often allude to the Bible, for instance, or to fairy tales or other well-known works. Many contemporary poets make allusions to movies or to popular songs.

To use allusions well, you need to know your audience. If you are writing for your peers, you can expect them to know certain musical groups, music, books, and television shows with which your parents, your teachers, and other older adults might not be familiar. Not everyone needs to understand everything in your poems. But give some thought to your audience before you make an allusion to something only you and a few friends know.

USING FIGURATIVE LANGUAGE IN YOUR POEM

Good figurative language is concrete, condensed, and interesting. It should be suited to the mood and tone of the poem you are writing. You probably wouldn't want to compare a sunset to a bloody wound if you were writing a lyrical poem about tenderness. Nor, in a poem of war and violence would you compare a bloody wound to the opening of a rosebud. On the other hand, you might—it would depend on what you are trying to communicate.

REVISION

Look again at the rough draft of your poem to make sure you have made the best use of figures of speech.

- *Comparisons*

Have you made any comparisons? Did you use *like* or *as* or is the comparison a metaphor? If you used a simile, try making it a metaphor. If you used a metaphor, try it as a simile. Which works better?

Are your comparisons fresh or are some clichés? Can you strengthen them by changing a word or two, or the entire comparison?

Have you compared abstract to concrete or concrete to concrete?

If you haven't used any comparisons, are there places where they would help you to make your meaning clearer?

See if you can work one simile or one metaphor into your poem.

Try to compare concrete to concrete.

- *Personification*

Have you used personification in your poem?

Have you treated a thing as if it were a person?

Do inanimate objects speak or move in ways only a living creature could actually speak or move?

Does the personification work for you? Or is it trite?

Does it convey the feeling and tone you want to communicate to your reader at that point in the poem?

- *Symbols*

  Are there any symbols in your poem?
  If so, what is the literal thing, and what does it stand for?
  Is the symbol used well—is it engaging and interesting, or trite?

- *Other Figures*

  Have you used metonymy? Synecdoche?
  Could you?
  Is there a part you could substitute for the whole, or vice versa?
  Is there something you could name by substituting something related to it?

FINALLY

Go through your poem again and remove any clichés; replace them with fresh concrete images or comparisons.

SEVEN

SOUND

Poetry is music in words.

—Dr. Fuller

To hear the music of poetry, begin with one of your favorite poems, preferably a poem written by a published author, not something you've written yourself. If you don't have a favorite poem or doubt your own taste, choose something by Robert Frost, W. B. Yeats, Sylvia Plath, John Keats, Wallace Stevens, Marianne Moore, or Elizabeth Bishop. Then read the poem you've chosen aloud and really listen to how it sounds.

You might want to tape-record your reading of the poem, so that you can listen to it without looking at it. Can you hear the music of the words? Do particular sounds or patterns of sounds attract and engage you? Are there any unpleasant sounds? Does the poem, as a whole or in particular places, sound like what it's saying?

Now, working with a copy of the poem (either retype it or use a copy machine) read through it again. Notice the vowels (*A*, *E*, *I*, *O*, *U*) or vowel combinations (*EA, AE, OU, OI,* etc.) that are repeated. Does the poet repeatedly use a long *A* sound or the short *E* sound, for example, in the same or adjoining lines? If so, mark them.

Are there consonants that recur throughout the poem—a pattern of *P*s or *B*s, lots of *K*s or *R*s? Mark these, too, preferably in a different color.

Are there any rhymes in the poem? Do they occur at the ends of lines or within lines? You can mark these by assigning a letter to each sound. For instance, if the first line ends in the word *ear*, mark that sound as *a*. Let's say the next line ends in the word *afraid*. Mark that sound as *b*. If the next end word is *clear*, mark that *a* again, because it rhymes with *ear*. Continue through the poem, assigning each new sound a different letter of the alphabet and repeating letters each time a sound repeats.

Read the poem aloud again and notice how it feels to recite it. Is it easy to say or are there some tongue twisters embedded in it? Mark any word, or series of words, you find difficult to pronounce.

Once you've performed this exercise on a poem written by another poet, go back to your draft poem— the poem you are working on—and do the same thing. First, read your poem aloud and pay attention to how it sounds. Then mark recurring patterns of sound, including vowel sounds, consonant sounds, and rhymes. Then read your poem aloud once more to see if there are any words or groups of words that are difficult to pronounce.

SEEING AND HEARING SOUND PATTERNS

Don't be surprised if the first poem—the one written by another poet—is a web of repeated sounds. Poets pay a great deal of attention to the music of the words they use. Rhyme is the most obvious sonic device poets use, but there are many others.

For example, look at the first three lines of this poem, called "Braiding My Daughter's Hair":

Your dark gold hair hangs halfway down
*   your back.*
Each night you nestle in my lap
and let me braid it up. Daddy picks the book.

Notice the repetition of the *A* sound in the first and second lines. Then note the repeated *K* sounds (dark, back, picks, book,) the *B* sounds (back, braid, book), the *P* sounds (lap, up, picks,) the *R*s (your, dark, hair), the *H*s (hair, hangs, halfway). Although the three lines do not rhyme, they are musical. Sound holds the stanza together, interweaving the words and lines the way the speaker is braiding strands of hair.

Poets, including you, can use sound—rhyme and off rhyme, assonance and consonance, and onomatopoeia—to engage the senses and to help communicate feelings.

THE USES OF RHYME

Scientists are investigating the fact that most parents chatter away in doggerel to their children. And many of the most popular children's books—from Mother Goose's to Dr. Seuss's—are written in rhyming verse. A recent article in the *New York Times* pointed out that national myths are often put into rhyme: "One if by land, two if by sea, and I on the opposite shore will be." And we use rhyme to drive sayings into memory. The popular and memorable chant of 1960s anti war demonstrators, for example, gained power through rhyme: "Hey, hey, LBJ, how many kids did you kill today?"

Rhyme is not necessarily the mark of poetry, though many people associate poetry and rhyme.

Greeting-card writers use rhyme. Advertisers use rhyme to help plant a product's name in consumers' minds, hoping it will pop up in memory as those consumers cruise the supermarket aisles.

Reading specialists also use rhyme to help identify children who are ready to read. About 80 percent of kindergartners will easily find three words that rhyme with cat. "The other struggling 20 percent are heading toward difficulties that will require remediation," the *Times* article stated.

The urge to rhyme, and the reason for rhyme, cut across linguistic barriers. Children in Russia, in Italy, in Japan, in countries all around the world, love rhyme.

Rap artists declaim in rhyme, and gifted speakers often use rhyme in their presentations. Rhyme is even a way to help remember the forms of irregular English verbs, such as "ring, rang, rung," or "sing, sang, sung," and the facts of the calendar: "Thirty days hath September, April, June, and November."

Scientists have several theories about why humans find rhyme almost universally pleasurable. The most popular theory is that rhyme, because it gives shape to speech and creates patterns of sound, simplifies the world. And human beings find patterns very pleasing—whether those patterns are stripes and plaids, or periodic and harmonious sounds.

SOUND OR SENSE?

The sound of poetry is clearly a source of pleasure. Syllables arranged in a harmonious pattern are satisfying and pleasing, even if they mean little or nothing. The poem "Jabberwocky" by Lewis Carroll, which begins, "Twas brillig, and the slithy toves / did gyre and gimbel in the wabes," is enjoyable for its sound alone, and for its mere suggestion of sense. Jazz musicians who sing scat—jazz singing with nonsense syllables—also give great pleasure to their audiences.

Some people think that the sound pattern of a poem is primary and that the meaning of the words is secondary and a somewhat inferior form of pleasure. Others say that beginning poets should work primarily without rhyme, because rhyme is difficult to use well.

Certainly, rhyme can make a poem resonate, echoing in the air, in the ear, and in the mind, but writing in rhyme can cause beginning writers to stray too far from sense, especially if they have excellent ears and are facile versifiers. On the other hand, if rhyming is done with rigor, it can help a beginning poet discover fresh words and new areas of meaning. In addition, rhyme ties a poem to a strong English poetic tradition.

There's really no reason to use rhyme either all the time, or never. Try it when it suits you, and let it go if it's a bother. Attempting to find perfect rhymes can keep a beginning poet superficial, and sometimes, in the quest for rhyme, a young poet sacrifices meaning and the truth of an experience.

In the early stages of writing poetry, it's perhaps better to see the extraordinary in the ordinary, and express that clearly, than to rhyme. But in poetry, both sound and sense matter, and good poets use both, working together, to convey what they feel. It is the marriage of sound with emotional truth, insight, and all the other tools of poetry that contributes to the power of your work.

KINDS OF RHYME

Rhymed words end in corresponding sounds. *Moon*, *June*, and *spoon* all end in the *oon* sound, so we say they rhyme. What's more, we say these words have exact, or *perfect rhyme*, because they end in the exact same sound.

If you choose to use perfect rhyme in a poem, you really should use perfect rhyme throughout. Once you rhyme the first four lines, for example, your reader is going to expect the rhyming pattern to continue in that pattern throughout the poem. Technically, it's considered best not to pair the singular of a word (*tree*) with the plural of its rhyming partner (*seas*) in perfect rhyme.

One problem with using rhyme in English is the limited range of words available. Make sure to stay away from those words (such as *moon*, *spoon*, and *June*) that have been linked so often the reader can predict what the next one will be. Try to introduce an element of surprise into the rhyme scheme: *elephant* with *content* with *element*, for example, might make an interesting set of rhyming words to work with.

Rhymed poems should sound modern. Don't reach back into the past for words that rhyme but write with colloquial diction—the language of everyday life. This will save your rhymed poems from sounding musty, or worse still, like bad imitations of the worst Victorian verse.

And, if you choose to use rhyme, don't think rhyme is enough to carry the poem. Your work will still need to be concrete, to use imagery or figures of speech, and to appeal to the senses.

OFF RHYME

Another kind of rhyme goes by various names. *Off rhyme*, *slant rhyme*, *near rhyme*, and *half rhyme* are variously defined, but they amount to much the same thing. In this kind of rhyme, the final consonant sounds match, but the vowels differ. *Soul* and *oil*, and *mirth* and *forth* are two sets of off rhymes.

English is not as full of perfect rhymes as are Spanish, French, and Italian, because English is not an inflected language—we don't change the endings of a noun every time we use it differently in a sentence. Whether *farmer* is the subject of a sentence (The farmer fell) or the object of the sentence (He hit the farmer), we use the same form—*farmer*.

Inflected languages, on the other hand, add different endings to words depending upon where the word appears in the sentence and the kind of work it does. In Latin, for example, the farmer who does the action, the subject of the sentence, would be *agricola*, while the farmer who received the action and was the object of the sentence would be *agricolam*. Because you add the same endings to many different words, many words could, potentially, rhyme.

Using off rhyme gives the poet writing in English access to a much wider rhyming vocabulary. The choice of words is broader, and it's possible to make the music of the poem more subtle than the constant chiming of perfect rhymes. Half rhymes or slant rhymes allow for more modulations.

American poet Emily Dickinson was a master of off rhyme and used it in many of her poems. She would rhyme *firm* with *room*, for example, *tell* with *still*, *pearl* with *alcohol*. Dickinson's rhymes are generally termed *slant rhymes*. It was an innovation editors in her lifetime and immediately after her death didn't quite understand. In fact, some early editors thought Dickinson's off rhyme a sign that the poet had a tin ear and sometimes edited her work to make it rhyme perfectly.

Like dissonance in modern music, slant rhyme takes a little getting used to, but it can be a very exciting musical tool. One contemporary poet who uses slant rhyme exquisitely is Mona Van Duyn.

Emily Dickinson's innovative and daring use of off rhyme confounded critics of the time.

EYE RHYME

A third kind of rhyme possible in English is called *eye rhyme.*

The English language has many words that look like they should rhyme but are, in fact, pronounced quite differently. *Bough, enough,* and *cough* look like they should sound the same but do not. These words, if used together in a poem, would be called eye rhymes.

PLACING RHYMES

Where you place a rhyme matters. You can, for example, use *end rhyme*:

> *I think that I shall never see*
> *A poem lovely as a tree.*
> *A tree that may in summer wear*
> *A nest of robins in her hair.*
>
> (Joyce Kilmer)

End rhymes are one of the main ways in which stanzas and poetic forms, such as the sonnet, are constructed. (For additional information on writing in forms, see chapter ten). In the example above, each line has eight syllables, and the last word of each line rhymes.

Internal rhyme means the rhymes take place within the lines themselves, not at the end. Yet, we tend to hear rhymes as the end of lines. When the rhymes are closer together, they give the impression of shorter lines. This can make it feel as if the poem is moving faster. The internal rhymes work almost against, or in counterpoint to, the length of the lines. For the reader, there is a subtle pull, like something you might hear in Bach. For the listener, unless the reader of the poem is expert, the counterpoint is lost. It merely sounds like shorter lines, a quicker pace. For an example of a poem which makes excellent use of internal rhyme, see "Thee and Lew Freemen" by Cynthia Zarin.

RHYME SCHEMES

Rhyme schemes are the patterns in which rhymes appear in a poem. For instance, we would say that the following lines have a rhyme scheme of *aabb*:

> *I think that I shall never see* (a)
> *A poem lovely as a tree.* (a)
> *A tree that may in summer wear* (b)
> *A nest of robins in her hair.* (b)

A rhyme scheme is usually set in the first stanza of a poem. After that stanza, the reader expects all following stanzas to follow the same rhyme scheme or pattern of rhyming. If the rest of the poem quoted above stopped rhyming altogether, or began to rhyme *cdeffedc*, the reader might be confused. Instead, he or she would expect to see, and hear, *ccddee*, and so on.

If you establish a rhyme scheme in your poem, stick to it. It will only confuse your reader if you are constantly switching schemes.

ALLITERATION

Alliteration is the repetition of initial consonants. The tongue twister "Peter Piper picked a peck of pickled peppers," for instance, makes excessive use of alliteration. Every word begins with the letter *P*.

It's easy to use alliteration; it's something speech-writers love to do. William Safire, for instance, who wrote speeches for the Nixon/Agnew administration, invented many phrases deriding the intellectuals of the nation and relied on alliteration to make them stick in the minds of the audience, such as the phrase "nattering nabobs of negativity."

Although alliteration is easy to use, it's also easy to misuse and challenging to use well. A powerful technique, it has roots in English poetry.

Early Anglo-Saxon poetry was strongly alliterative. And although rhyme—end sounds that correspond—is more common in inflected languages, such as French and Italian, than in English—alliteration seems natural to English. In English, many words begin with the same letter.

Anglo-Saxon poetry, such as *Beowulf*, and the poems of early English writers, such as Geoffrey Chaucer, rely heavily on alliteration. Contemporary poets use alliteration as a sonic device, too; look especially at the work of W. H. Auden. And many common English phrases—*bread and butter*, *ticker tape*, *snowsuit*, *firefighter*—make use of the alliterative nature of the language. In fact, the love of alliteration has never left English, though it did, for a while, become subordinate to end rhyme.

If you are using alliteration in a poem, the most important thing to control is the pacing—the period of time that elapses between the words that begin with the same letter. You don't want the identical initial consonants to occur so close together that they pile up and create a tongue twister. You do want them close enough together so that they create an effect.

Experiment with alliteration to see what distance between words works best. In general, it's better to understate the alliteration rather than to overdo it.

ASSONANCE

Assonance is the repetition of vowel sounds. Some say that consonants are the skeleton of a word, giving it its physical identity, and that vowels represent the spirit of the word.

Handling vowel sounds well is one of the most important and subtle techniques of poetry in English. How you do this makes an enormous difference in the musicality of your verse.

For example, look at these last lines of a poem that appeared in the *Hudson Review*:

> *How strange it is*
> *to hover over words, like the smoke*
> *from the loggers' fires, over the valley.*
> (Nina Bogan, "March 1992")

Notice how many *O* sounds occur in these few lines: how, to, hover, over, smoke, from, loggers, over. You most likely didn't notice this play with the *O* sound as you read the lines, but the subtle shifts and repetitions are responsible for the music and power of these seemingly simple lines.

ONOMATOPOEIA

In his poem "Essay on Criticism" Alexander Pope talks about and uses many techniques of poetry. A famous line, "The sound must seem an echo to the sense," goes right to the heart of defining onomatopoeia.

Our language can quite successfully mimic the sounds it is describing. When words recreate the sounds they describe, it's called *onomatopoeia*. Words like *buzz*, *hum*, *clank*, and *crash* are onomatopoeic words. A line often cited as an example of onomatopoeia is from Tennyson's "Requiem": "Break, break break on your cold gray stones, o sea." The repetition of the word *break* mimics the continual breaking of waves on rocks. Another Tennyson line, "murmuring of innumerable bees," creates the kind of buzzing and humming sound, the murmur, about which the line is talking.

Keats is another master of onomatopoeia. He describes musk roses as the "murmurous haunts of flies on summers eves," and we can hear the sound of the flies as we read the line.

REVISION: MAKING SOUND WORK FOR YOU

Go back again to that draft of your poem, the one where you marked repeated consonants, vowel sounds, rhymes, and other sonic devices.

Have you used rhyme? Is it perfect, off or slant, or a combination? Do you begin a rhyme scheme and then abandon it? Could you either drop the rhyme scheme, strengthen it, or change it, to the improvement of your poem? Are there sounds you want to make more of within the poem?

Look for synonyms—words that mean the same or something close to the word you've used in your poem. Perhaps you can find a word that works better musically, but which means almost exactly the same thing:

Clearly the lake is too big.
vs.
Clearly the lake is too large.

The change of one word, *big* to *large*, makes a tremendous difference in the musicality of the line.

Have you used assonance and/or alliteration in your poem? Have you used them well, or could you improve on them? If you haven't used these techniques of sound, can you revise the poem to include at least one instance of each?

Onomatopoeia isn't right for every poem. But if you are trying to communicate what something sounds like within the poem, perhaps you should try to write a line that is strictly onomatopoeic. In fact, why not write a line that sounds like what it's saying, just for practice, and see if you can write another poem to go with it.

If you find that making your poem more musical is difficult, don't despair. Although some people have more natural musical talent than others, everyone's ability to make a poem more lyrical can be improved by attention and practice.

Pay attention to the music of language in the speech around you, in everything you read, and in your prose writing as well as your poetry. Soon enough, your ear will become attuned to the music of words, and you will begin to write musically, even when you are in the grip of an idea and trying to get it down, hot, into the shape of a poem.

EIGHT

RHYTHM AND METER

It Don't Mean a Thing If It Ain't Got That Swing
—Duke Ellington (Song Title, 1932)

Great metrical achievement, on its own, does not make great poetry.
—Paul Fussell, *Poetic Meter and Poetic Form*

Rhythm is intrinsic and essential to poetry. All poems have rhythm, because all language, including everyday speech, has rhythm. It's possible to have a poem without rhyme, but it's not possible to have a poem without rhythm. In fact, there are some who say that attempts to escape from meter amount to attempts to escape from poetry itself.

Some poems—free verse, for instance—work by highlighting and heightening the natural rhythms of speech. Other poems—sonnets, for example—are based on a formal metrical pattern.

LEARNING ABOUT RHYTHM

In *The ABC of Reading*, Ezra Pound calls attention to the importance of rhythm in poetry: "poetry begins to atrophy when it gets too far from music." If you know anything about music, you know something about rhythm. *Rhythm* is the underlying pattern of stresses and accents. It's the pulse of music that allows you to "keep time."

Do you find yourself tapping your foot as you listen to music? You are tuned in to the rhythm of the piece. Rhythm is what you follow when you're dancing—not the melody or the tune, but the underlying pattern of stressed or accented notes. Rhythm is, quite simply, the beat.

Rhythm is not the only way we "keep" time—it is a way in which we order time. Pound wrote that "rhythm is a form cut in time, as a design is determined space." Creating rhythm is a very natural impulse and can be as pleasurable as rhyming. Even when sounds don't have a rhythm, we tend to impose one. A clock, for instance, makes only a single sound— *tick, tick, tick*—over and over. Yet as we listen, we add an accent and create a rhythm: *tick tock, tick tock, tick tock.*

Perhaps we like rhythm so much because we embody it. Listen quietly, and you will hear the rhythm of your own heartbeat. Pay attention to the rhythm of your breathing. Walk, run, or dance and feel the rhythm as you move your legs and feet. Rhythm is natural to us. We celebrate it in our bodies, as well as in poetry and song.

RHYTHM IN POETRY

In poetry, rhythm is the rise and fall, the swelling and subsiding, of words. It is the beat of the poem, the

96

pattern of stresses or accents, that underlies the words the poet uses.

The best way to learn the music of verse is to listen to it. Read some of your favorite poems aloud and listen for the rhythm. Is it slow or fast? If you were dancing to the poem, what kind of dance would you do—a rhumba, a samba, a waltz, a two-step, the hustle, or the frug?

See if you can find two poems with wildly different rhythms. Compare, for example, a Theodore Roethke poem about dancing with a Cornelius Eady poem from his book *Victims of the Latest Dance Craze*. Compare the rhythms of Shakespeare with the rhythms of Frank O'Hara, or the rhythms of Walt Whitman with those of Emily Dickinson.

If you're interested in writing rap poems, read and listen to rap. If it's iambic pentameter you're after, read and listen to the plays of Shakespeare or rent videos of Shakespeare's plays. Whatever you choose, immerse yourself in it and let yourself experience the rhythms.

It's a good idea, too, to read some poems where the rhythm is very regular, and possibly even poems written with a heavy hand. These are not to be imitated, of course, but they should give you a feeling of the beat of a poem, and how boring rhythm can be if it's never or rarely varied. Try a few stanzas of an old standard, such as "Casey at the Bat," by Ernest Lawrence Thayer or anything by Edgar Guest.

Look at some free verse, too, and listen for its rhythms. One of the best writers of free verse, whom W. H. Auden claimed had an almost infallible ear, is D. H. Lawrence. Read a few of his poems aloud, and you will hear how the rhythms of speech can be heightened and accentuated to the point where they become almost music.

BACK TO YOUR POEM

Now look at your draft and read it aloud. With your ears tuned to the rhythms of other poets, what kind of music do you hear in what you have written? Is it a dance tune, a march, the repeated banging of a drum? Have you used a regular rhythm? Or did you employ free verse, the native rhythms of speech?

You can get a general sense of the kind of rhythm you've used just by listening, but to conduct a serious analysis of what's going on in a poem rhythmically, it's helpful to learn some of the terms and techniques of scansion—analyzing verse to show its meter. To do that, you'll first need to know some technical terms that describe various kinds of meters.

METER

Meter is rhythm that is measured and counted—that is, rhythm arranged and shaped into a pattern. Just as musical compositions are usually written in a specific meter—4/4 time, or 3/4 time, for example—many poems are written in a specific meter: *iambic*, *trochaic*, *dactylic*, or *anapestic*.

The meter of poetry is an important part of a poem's message. It conveys physical and emotional information that help the words convey more information than they would without it. Organizing language metrically is part of the universal human impulse towards order. Lines of poetry constantly remind us that they have a pattern; meter puts the stresses of rhythm at regular intervals.

Meter is the most basic way available to the poet of imposing order on language. It results when the natural rhythmical movements of everyday speech are heightened, organized, and regulated so that a pattern becomes clear. Pattern, by the way, is made through repetition. Having stresses in a poem recur at regular intervals creates the pattern of meter.

Meter was probably first used as a way to help remember bits of wisdom and lore. When used for this purpose, it's important that the meter be as regular and singsong as possible. These meters, though easy to remember, are not particularly subtle or expressive:

Monday's child is fair of face.
Tuesday's child is full of grace...

Think of a poem's meter as its heartbeat, or pulse. Most of the time there will be a steady, even beat. But meter—like a pulse—will vary when feelings run high (excitement, anger, passion, and more) or are dulled (depression, sorrow, exhaustion, boredom, for example). By varying meter, a poet can reinforce emotional effects.

Meter also adds meaning to poems by means of association and convention. Limericks, for example, have a particular meter that seems to suggest wicked wit and impudence, if not obscenity. Whether by long association or by intrinsic physical feel, the meter of the limerick has meaning even without words.

Recite the rhythm of a limerick, substituting *ta-tum* for the words, and you'll see. Put the stress, or accent, on the syllable *tum*:

ta tum ta ta tum ta ta tum ta
ta tum ta ta tum ta ta tum ta
ta tum ta ta tum
ta tum ta ta tum
ta tum ta ta tum ta ta tum ta

WHAT DOES METER MEASURE?

The word *meter* comes to English (through Old French and Latin) from the Greek word meaning *measure*. To understand and use meter, it's important to know what you're measuring. As a general rule, the meter of a language measures the most conspicuous phonetic characteristic of that language. It could be the number of syllables, the number of accents, the number of accents and syllables, or the length of each syllable. In poetry written in English, we usually measure the number of accents (stressed syllables) as well as the number of syllables (the smallest unit of spoken language) in a line.

Stress is the vocal emphasis with which a syllable is spoken, relative to the emphasis given to the syllables that lie on either side of it. So, for example, in the word *explosion* the stress or accent is on the second syllable, *plo*, because it is emphasized more than the other two syllables when we pronounce it.

Not every word must have an accent. In English, many short words are not stressed at all, and are heard like prefixes or suffixes. In the following line, for example, there are many small unaccented words:

When Í hăve feárs thăt Í mĭght ceáse tŏ bé
(John Keats, "When I Have Fears")

FEET

The foot is the basic unit of measuring rhythm in English. It consists of two or three syllables, one of which is stressed. The repetition of the foot throughout the poem creates a more or less regular pattern of stresses (the meter) from which the poet may stray to make a point or to create some variety. To understand the overall pattern of a line, it helps to know the feet used to measure meter. There are six basic feet in English:

Iambs

The *iamb* or *iambic foot* consists of an unstressed syllable followed by a stressed syllable. You can hear the iamb at work in the following words: com**plete**, be**half**, con**demn**, re**peat**, in**vite**, al**low**.

Iambic meter is the most common in English poetry, probably because English is, by its nature, iambic. Our language seems to work most comfortably in rising rhythms, and iambic rhythms most closely resemble the heightening of natural speech.

Trochees

The *trochee* is a two-syllable foot in which the first syllable is accented. You might think of the trochee as the opposite of an iamb.

Many common English phrases are trochaic: bread and butter; bread and water.

Trochees are an unusual choice for the main meter of a poem; far more poems are written in iambs than in trochees. The falling rhythm of the trochee is not as close to the normal speech patterns of English, so that trochees tend to sound very distinctive when used as the chief meter of a poem, and perhaps a little bit forced.

The Henry Wadsworth Longfellow poem *The Song of Hiawatha*, for example, which begins, "By the shores of Gitche Gumee,..." is written largely in trochaic meter. The trochees create the effect of beating tom-toms, providing a kind of underlying drumbeat. But the rhythm and meter are so distinctive and insistent that, at times, they steal center stage. The meaning of the words becomes subordinate to the rhythm.

More often than they are used as the base meter of an English poem, trochees appear as substitutions in iambic lines. When used in an iambic context, a trochee conveys the effect of sudden movement or surprise. Trochees are often introduced by means of an active verb in the first foot of an iambic line, giving the feeling of sudden force or violence:

Tíe up̆ thĕ knóckĕr, sáy I'm̆ sĭck, I'm̆ deád.
(Alexander Pope, "Epistle to Dr. Arbuthnot")

Dańce, ănd Pr̆ovéncăl sóng, ănd
sŭnbur̆nt mírth!…
(John Keats, "Ode to a Nightingale")

When a trochee is used at the end of a line it can reinforce a feeling of sincerity or be a trigger for irony. Keats—who had tuberculosis and died at the age of twenty-six—often used a trochee to end an iambic line when he was writing about love that he would never experience.

Anapests

The *anapest* is a foot of three syllables, two unaccented syllables followed by an accented syllable. Perhaps you know the famous poem by Clement Moore that is written largely in anapestic meter:

'Tw̆ăs thĕ níght bĕfŏre Christm̆as ănd áll
thróugh thĕ hoúse
Nŏt ă créatŭre wăs stírriñg nŏt évĕn ă moúse.
Thĕ stóckiñgs wĕre húng by̆ thĕ chímn̆ey
wĭth care
Ĭn hope thăt St̆. Níchŏlăs soón wŏuld bĕ thére.

Dactyls

A dactyl is a foot of three syllables in which the first syllable is accented and the last two syllables are unaccented. *Violence*, *pulchritude*, and *liniment* are all dactylic words. Longfellow's poem "Evangeline" is written in dactylic meter:

Thís ĭš thĕ fořešt prĭmévăl. Thĕ múrmŭriňg
  pinés aňd thĕ hémločks,
Beárdĕd wĭth móss, aňd iň gármĕnts grĕen,
  iňdĭstiňct iň thĕ twĭliğht,
Staňd liǩe Dřuidš óf elđ, wĭth vóicĕs sád
  aňd přophétic,

Spondees

A *spondee* or *spondaic foot* consists of two syllables, both of which are accented:

Thăt Í shăll névĕr lóok ŭpón thēe mōre...
  (John Keats, "When I Have Fears")

Ťo wálk aňd páss oŭr loňg loǿe's dáy.
  (Andrew Marvell, "To His Coy Mistress")

Notice how the spondee seems to stretch time, to slow down the movement of the poem.

Pyrrhics

Feet of two syllables which have no accent are called *pyrrhics*. Because they do not have a stress, pyrrhics are often not considered legitimate feet in English.

LINE LENGTHS

Lines in English poetry are named by a combination of the accentual pattern and the number of feet in a line:

Monometer—one foot
Dimeter—two feet
Trimeter—three feet

Tetrameter—four feet
Pentameter—five feet
Hexameter—six feet
Heptameter—seven feet
Octameter—eight feet

We describe lines of poetry by the kind and number of feet they contain. So a line with five iambic feet is called *iambic pentameter*; a line with three dactylic feet is called *dactylic trimeter*.

SCANSION

Scansion is a system that uses visual symbols to represent conventional poetic rhythms so that we can analyze and discuss them. Scanning a poem reveals its meter.

To scan a line, or an entire poem, read it through, and mark stressed or accented syllables with a line like this: /. Mark unstressed or less stressed syllables with a mark like this: ˇ.

You will soon notice that feet don't always correspond with the words in a poem. Metrical feet are like the bars in music; they do not necessarily coincide with the unit of a phrase.

Nor does the grammar and sense of each line have to end when the line ends. In fact, it would be awfully boring if every line and every sentence ended together, in what's called *end-stopped* lines. Better, by far, to vary the endings. Sometimes the end of a line will be the end of a natural grammatical unit. Sometimes, the sentence will run on through several lines. These lines are called run-on lines, or *run-ons*. Look at the opening lines of Robert Frost's famous poem "Mending Wall" to see how a master varies end-stopped and run-on lines.

MENDING WALL
Robert Frost

Something there is that doesn't love a wall,
That sends the frozen-ground-swell under it
And spills the upper boulders in the sun,
And makes gaps even two can pass abreast.
The work of hunters is another thing:
I have come after them and made repair
Where they have left not one stone on a stone
But they would have the rabbit out of hiding
To please the yelping dogs. The gaps I mean,
No one has seen them or heard them made,
But at spring mending-time we find them there.

Be aware, too, that while there is an ideal metrical scheme underlying many poems—perfect iambic pentameter, say—the real metrical scheme will be somewhat different. The distance between the ideal meter and the real meter embodied in the words the poet chooses creates a certain amount of tension— and in this tension lies much music, and poetry.

IAMBIC PENTAMETER

English and American poetry offer a number of inherited metrical forms that have been used again and again. Perhaps the most widely used is iambic pentameter.

In poetry written in English, iambic lines are, most commonly, five feet long. Iambic pentameter lines are a staple of English poetry. Why should you consider writing in a metrical form that is so old, so accepted, so timeworn?

Well, compare the inherited form to a proven, time-tested recipe—say, the recipe for basic chocolate chip cookies. Who cares if the recipe is old? The cookies are always delicious. And once you've learned to make them, you can always alter the recipe a little, adding pecans instead of walnuts, tossing in a handful of raisins or a spoonful or two or grated orange rind, giving the old standby your own personal touch.

As with cookies, so with meter. A basic, inherited, time-tested form such as iambic pentameter provides a structure through which you can learn to write in meter. Later, once you've perfected it, you can learn to create your own unique variations.

The basic pattern, which proceeds:

ta tum ta tum ta tum ta tum ta tum

can give way to hundreds of different variations:

Shall I compare thee to a summer's day?

Look at Milton's *Paradise Lost*, the odes of Wordsworth and Keats, the sonnets and verse dramas of Shakespeare to get a sense of the possibilities of iambic pentameter.

Of course, the iambic line can also be used to convey satire and irony, which are, in fact, very serious subjects. And so we find the satiric works of Pope written in iambics as well.

What dire offense from amorous causes springs,
What mighty contests rise from trivial things,
    (Alexander Pope, "The Rape of the Lock")

Such lines are also called heroic couplets—two lines of iambic pentameter that rhyme with each other.

Unrhymed iambic pentameter is also called blank verse, the form Milton used for *Paradise Lost*:

William Shakespeare's verse has inspired poets and readers throughout the world for hundreds of years.

Of man's first disobedience, and the fruit
of that forbidden tree, whose mortal taste
brought death into the world, and all our woe
with loss of Eden, till one greater Man
restore us, and regain our blissful seat,
sing, heavenly Muse!

You could spend a lifetime—many people have—studying iambic pentameter. For a poet's purposes, however, there are two important ways to study it: read it and write it.

Try writing twenty lines of unrhymed iambic pentameter. See if you can tell a story. Play with the placement of accents and discover what you like and what you don't like when you make changes in the lines.

Then try writing a short poem—perhaps ten to twenty lines—in heroic couplets.

HINTS ON USING METER

In great poetry, the meter matches the mood of the poem. It will, in other words, appear natural and unforced. Any effort by the poet to align the meter with the meaning will be hidden.

One way to make sure your meter sounds unforced is to read it aloud as many times as needed and make adjustments in words and the order of phrases until the poem sounds right. (Achieving a sense of what sounds right requires continuous reading of metrically excellent poetry.)

Be careful, though, when rearranging words and phrases to heighten a metrical pattern. Contemporary poetry favors natural word order; in English, that's usually subject—verb—object. Don't twist your syntax into pretzels in order to achieve a metrical effect. If your lines won't flow into iambic pentameter, you may want to consider free verse (see next chapter).

Every poem, from the first few words, creates metrical expectations within the reader. Poet and critic John Hollander calls this "the metrical contract." He means that, from the first few words, the poet and the reader agree that a certain meter in the poem will prevail. Subtle variations in the meter will add much interest, but most of the poem should be written in the meter set out in the first few words. Freedom is not a virtue in meter; expressiveness is.

What kind of variations will help to create that expressiveness? Well, try a succession of stressed syllables when you want to create a sense of slowness, weight, or difficulty. A series of unstressed syllables will give you the opposite effect: a sense of rapidity and lightness.

You can reverse the rhythm (beginning a line with a trochee instead of an iamb, for instance) to indicate sudden movement, discovery, or illumination. A shift in rhythm can also indicate that the poem is taking a fresh direction or that, after some insight or climax, the poet is using a new tone of voice, a different level of intensity.

> *Darkling I listen, and for many a time*
> *I have been half in love, with easeful death, ...*
>   (John Keats, "Ode to a Nightingale")

Another tool that poets use to make metrical lines more natural sounding and more varied is called the *caesura*. This is a natural break, sort of a breath, taken within the line of verse. It is a pause, not as strong as the pause felt at the end of a line, but a pause nonetheless. By varying the placement of the caesura from line to line, the poet can create a counterpoint, a different rhythm within the agreed-to plan. In scanning a poem, the caesura is marked with a double vertical line, like so:

> *Darkling I listen, ‖ and for many a time*
> *I have been half in love ‖ with easeful death, ...*
>   (John Keats, "Ode to a Nightingale")

Of man's first disobedience, || and the fruit
of the forbidden tree, || whose mortal taste
brought death into the world, || and all our woe
(John Milton, *Paradise Lost*)

What lips my lips have kissed, || and where, ||
   and why
I have forgotten....
(Edna St. Vincent Millay, "Sonnet")

REVISION

Take a look at your draft from a rhythm and meter point of view. Copy your poem, or type it double spaced. Then scan the poem and mark the accented and unaccented syllables.

Look at your poem. Mark the metrical pattern. Have you used one kind of foot again and again? Would it make sense to use more of that foot, or to vary it?

Remember, the main metrical feet in English are:

*iamb—(de**stroy**)*
*trochee—(**top**sy)*
*anapest—(inter**vene**)*
*dactyl—(**mer**rily)*
*spondee—(**long love**)*
pyrrhic—two unaccented

Can you describe the predominant rhythmic pattern by the foot and the number of feet in the line? Would the poem be improved by heightening that pattern or by breaking free of it? Can you use different word choices—more concrete or more specific, for instance—to help create a stronger sense of rhythm and meter in your poem?

Consider what your poem is about. Is it primarily serious or largely comic? Does the rhythmic move-

110

ment of your poem echo the movement of the feeling? If not, how can you bring the movement into line?

Select a metrical pattern that most easily corresponds to your subject matter. If your poem is serious, satiric, or ironic, an iambic meter might help you to sharpen the tone. If your poem is about something joyful, comical, light—even superficial—a triple meter, built of anapests and dactyls, might help to convey the feeling you are after.

Have you end-stopped every line? Can you vary that to good effect?

Have you used pauses—caesuras—within lines? Are there places where you might do so?

A FINAL NOTE

Although meter and rhythm can be difficult to talk about, they are fairly easy to feel and to know intuitively. If the rhythm or meter of your poem isn't discernible to you, get help. Ask a parent, teacher, or classmate to read your work to you while you listen for, and perhaps mark, the stresses.

Just as some people seem to have a natural gift for dancing or playing a musical instrument, other people have a good ear for rhythm, meter, and accents. Don't be utterly discouraged if feeling and hearing the rhythm of a poem is difficult for you.

Remember that even musical prodigies don't learn to play an instrument in a single lesson. Writing well and rhythmically, in formal metrical patterns and free verse, is the result of reading, listening, and writing—again and again and again.

ꙍRMS, INCLUDING FREE VERSE

*Poetic forms…tend to say things even if words are
not at the moment fitted to their patterns.*
—Paul Fussell

*I think very few people can manage free verse.
You need an infallible ear, like D. H. Lawrence,
to determine where the lines should end.*
—W. H. Auden

All poems have form. There are those who claim that
poetry *is* form. Even the way a poem is arranged on
the page, with the poet, rather than the typesetter,
determining where one line ends and a new one
begins, confirms that poems have form and that form
is an important aspect of poetry.

There are poets who choose to write in traditional
forms and poets who make up their own forms as they
go along. Free verse is a form in which the subject matter of the poem is allowed to shape the way the poem
appears on the page. Free verse became extremely
popular during the early years of the twentieth century,

in part as a reaction against some very badly written formal poems circulating widely at the time.

Poets have a natural sense of the way that is best for them to write. It depends largely on the shape of their talent. Beat poet Allen Ginsberg writes in free verse, in long lines that are reminiscent of Whitman, whose work reflects the rolling passages of the King James Bible. A poet can begin with a pattern in mind or can work with language, images, and emotions until a pattern emerges.

WRITING IN FORM

People determine their personal form in a number of ways. When asked about the genesis of his poetry, about whether the form or the content came first, W. H. Auden replied:

> *At any given time I have two things on my mind—a theme that interests me, and a problem of verbal form. The theme looks for the right form; the form looks for the right theme. When the two come together, I am able to start writing.*

It is true that for most poets, poetry only happens at the intersection of form and subject matter. Still, there seem to be several methods by which poets decide to create a poem in a fixed form or set pattern:

- The poet decides (or is assigned) to write a poem in a given form. ("I will now write a villanelle." Or, "You will each write a sonnet; it's due by Friday.")
- The poet writes a few inspired lines and sees that the poem needs a form. A thirteen-, fourteen-, or fifteen-line poem may cry out to

be tidied up into a sonnet. A three-line stanza whose first and third lines have resonance may suggest to the poet a villanelle.

- The poet may look at the rough draft of a poem and the notes he or she has made and see that the material may work best as a villanelle, sonnet, or sestina.

There is nothing unnatural in our desire to find form and pattern in our experience. We like the reassurance of form; it sets boundaries and makes the world more orderly.

For the writer of poetry, form sets some limits on the almost endless possibilities of language. For in a fixed form, not just any word can end the line— but only one that ends with the appropriate sound may do so.

For the reader, a poem in a set form can feel like walking from room to room in a spacious house, rather than facing a prairie of endless grass and huge, distant horizons. Both are valuable, potentially pleasurable or enriching experiences. But they are different.

CONVERSATIONS WITH HISTORY

Have you ever seen a still-life painting—a painting featuring, perhaps, fruit, cheese, or a bottle of wine? The form of the still life has been used again and again. For a time it was largely an exercise, to assist painters in practicing to fool the eye—making painted grapes and glass appear translucent, for example, or painted fur appear soft and fluffy.

Some still-life paintings are masterpieces in their own right. And each one recalls and suggests every other still life we have ever seen. The painter of still lifes has entered into a conversation with history, commenting on all the other similar paintings by

The still life is a centuries-old form of painting used by artists as an exercise in perspective, texture, and tone.

what he or she chooses to include, exclude, highlight, or diminish.

When you choose to write in a conventional form—whether it's a sonnet, a rap song, or a haiku—it is similar to painting a still life. You begin a conversation with history. You are putting your poem in the tradition of all the other haiku, sonnets, or villanelles ever written and inviting your readers to compare and contrast yours with the others.

CHOOSING A FORM

To decide on the form before writing the poem may strike you as arbitrary or artificial. Couldn't the poem just grow naturally, like an apple or a zinnia, rather than being forced to follow a pattern?

It's an interesting question, because apples and zinnias, obviously, grow into set patterns. Otherwise, how would we know they were apples and zinnias?

Like an apple or a zinnia, a poem written in a form is likely to seem spontaneous. That's because you never see the poet crossing out, agonizing over word choice, returning to the draft again and again, hammering away at it until it is perfect. You see the easy, natural poem.

When you see a flawless figure-skating performance, you don't see the practicing and years of work it took to pull it off. Yet, you don't assume that the athlete just showed up and did it. Things that appear effortless almost always take the most work.

Artists, historically, have labored not to reveal the calculation and effort that went into their creations. Instead, the reader or viewer has been shown the ease and elegance of achievement, rather than the labor that went into it.

Of course, this is a matter of style. It is sometimes important to show the blows of the chisel, the mark of the brush, the struggle with language. Sometimes it's even fashionable. Still, you want those strokes, brushmarks, and struggles to be deliberate—and not a result of the fact that you, as creator, are totally out of control.

ORGANIZING: BY LINE OR BY STANZA?

Have you written a draft in which a sonnet is hiding? Is your draft a villanelle in disguise? How would you know?

Look over the draft of your poem. You will probably find that it is organized either into stanzas—groups of lines separated by space—or as a series of lines with no breaks.

Poets call the two ways of organizing or arranging poetry *strophic* (in stanzas) or *stichic* (by lines). A *stanza* is a group of lines set apart from the rest of the poem by space above and below. Strophes are stanzas that are irregular in shape.

Using stanzas can make a poem more inviting. Stanzas give the reader a visual shape to anticipate, a sense of how the poem might "taste," as the shape of a pear suggests its flavor. Stanzas can lure the eye into the poem or help the poem mimic the action it presents. Some poets adopt stanza forms for particular kinds of poems, as if to signal the reader. The odes of Wordsworth and Keats, for instance, each display a particular shape upon the page.

Which is the better way to arrange your poem on the page—strophic or stichic? It really depends on the poem, what it's about, and the effect you hope it will have on the reader. In general, strophes tend more toward song, and stichic poems tend more toward speech.

Some poems are repetitive—they detail a single state of mind that does not change. Others are narrative—they tell a story, and the sense of the unfolding action keeps the poem moving. Still other poems are built on the principles of logic and argument. "To His Coy Mistress," by Andrew Marvell, is a good example of a poem that is a logical argument.

Poems that are arranged by lines tend toward large, expansive, narrative, dramatic, or meditative actions. *Paradise Lost*, Milton's epic about the fall of Adam, is a stichic poem. Blank verse and free verse are generally stichic.

Poems that are arranged in strophes (stanzas), on the other hand, are more likely to deal with dense and limited moments of emotion, argument, or reminiscence. Stanzas function somewhat like paragraphs in prose: grouping like ideas and images together. Stanzas can be regular or irregular in shape.

REVIEWING YOUR DRAFT: FORM

Is it stichic or strophic? Are the strophes even, or irregular?

How does the shape relate to the meaning of the poem? Does the shape help or add anything to your meaning? Or does the shape in some way undercut your meaning?

If you have a block of lines, try breaking it up into stanzas. Does a stanza length suggest itself?

If your poem is in stanzas, try rewriting or typing it as a stichic poem. What, in your opinion, does your poem gain or lose by this exercise?

If you've written your twelve-line poem in four stanzas of three lines each, try it in three stanzas of four lines each. Does it need a couplet (a final two lines) to complete it?

NAMING STANZAS

How many lines should be in each stanza? You can have as few as two, or as many as fourteen—or more. Stanzas are named after the number of lines they contain:

Two-line stanza—couplet
Three-line stanza—tercet

Four-line—quatrain
Five-line—cinquain
Six-line—sestet
Eight-line—octave
Fourteen-line—sonnet

HOLDING A STANZA TOGETHER

Stanzas are ordinarily held together by end rhyme worked into rhyme schemes—a pattern of rhyme repeated in every stanza. Some forms are fairly common. The ballad, for example, is a four-line stanza, where the second and fourth lines rhyme. You can also write quatrains that rhyme *abab*, or *abba*.

Rhymes invite your reader to consider the similar meanings of words along with their similar sounds. That is why we speak of them holding the stanza together. Repeating the rhyme scheme in each stanza is another way to create a pattern through repetition. Some forms, such as sonnets, are created by combining stanzas.

THE ARCHITECTURE OF A SONNET

> *It takes a wealth of chaos in early life to produce a quest for order as emphatic as the one a sonnet imposes. Its severity creates a dense, closed world, one that begins where it ends...*
>
> —Molly Peacock

Literally thousands of sonnets, if not millions, have been written in English. So there is clearly something very satisfying in the proportions and design of a sonnet for both the writer and the reader.

If you would like to—or have to—write a sonnet, start by reading a few. You can find them in anthologies; many are titled, simply, "Sonnet." Or look into the sonnets of a particular poet: Keats, Millay, Shakespeare, e. e. cummings, or the work of other poets.

Scan a sonnet or two, and you'll quickly discover that sonnets are fourteen lines long and written in iambic pentameter. They differ, however, in their rhyme schemes and in their shapes.

The Italian or Petrachan sonnet is composed of an octave (eight-line section) and a sestet (six-line section). The octave is further subdivided into two four-line sections called quatrains, each rhyming *abba*. A new set of rhymes is used in the sestet, which can be rhymed in a number of patterns, such as *cdecde*. The Shakespearean, or English sonnet, on the other hand, is composed of three quatrains and a couplet.

The blueprints of the sonnets look like this:

Italian Sonnet

a			OCTAVE
b			
b			
a			
a			
b			
b			
a			
c	or	*c*	SESTET
d		*d*	
e		*c*	
c		*d*	
d		*c*	
e		*d*	

Example of an Italian sonnet from *A Crown of Sonnets*:

*We used to hunt each other. Now we meet
by accident, if we meet at all,
over blueberries in the produce stall,
or at our local butcher's, buying meat.
I'd like you to appear now, on this street,
in the old neighborhood. I would call
your name, suggest we breakfast without gall
at the Berkely Luncheonette. But would
   you eat?*

*Lying gestures cleared like dirty dishes,
silence cracked like eggs, we would sit down
reopening our friendship like a meal—
a rapprochement so stunning pigs and fishes
would know it in their bones.*
                  *You're not in town;
we both have wounds that talking would
   not heal.*

Shakespearean Sonnet

a	*QUATRAIN*
b	
a	
b	
c	*QUATRAIN*
d	
c	
d	
e	*QUATRAIN*
f	
e	
f	
g	*COUPLET*
g	

Example of a Shakespearean sonnet by William Shakespeare:

29

When in disgrace with fortune and men's eyes
I all alone beweep my outcast state,
And trouble deaf heaven with my bootless cries,
And look upon myself and curse my fate,
Wishing me like to one more rich in hope,
Featured like him, like him with friends possessed,
Desiring this man's art, and that man's scope,
With what I most enjoy, contented least;
Yet in these thoughts myself almost depising,
Haply I think on thee—and then my state,
Like to the lark at break of day arising
From sullen earth, sings hymns at heaven's gate;
*   For thy sweet love remembered, such wealth brings*
*   That then I scorn to change my state with kings.*

Although both are sonnets, the two forms have different structures. In the Italian sonnet, the introductory octave is slightly longer than the conclusion that happens in the sestet. The octave tends to be like an indrawn breath, the sestet like an exhalation or release.

In the English sonnet, the windup takes much longer—it's three quatrains instead of two. And the pitch—the exhale or release—is short and snappy. The poem has to unwind in two quick lines—that rhyme. And the poet has to cap off, summarize, or somehow top the twelve lines that have gone before it in this final couplet. This often gives the Shakespearean sonnet the feeling of having a punch line, like an O'Henry story.

THE OPENING

Sonnets have, in effect, a kind of architecture. As different rooms of a house are designed to accommodate dining, cooking, sleeping, and so on, different parts of a sonnet accommodate different actions.

Consider the Italian sonnet. In the first quatrain, (first four lines), the poet presents the subject. In the next four lines, the poet develops or complicates what has been set out above. For example, if you were writing a poem about your grandmother's house, you might show the reader the house in the first quatrain, and in the second quatrain begin to indicate that there are problems: perhaps the house is abandoned and falling down.

In a Shakespearean sonnet, a poet projects the subject in the first quatrain, complicates or develops it in the second, and further develops it in the third. It is challenging to develop the material further; Shakespearean sonnets are often weak in the third quatrain because the poet repeats, rather than expands on, what has already been said.

THE TURN

The *turn* in a sonnet is a logical or emotional shift by which the speaker is enabled to take a new, or altered, or enlarged view of the subject.

Italian and Shakespearean sonnets both have a turn, a point at which the problem or situation begins to be considered from a new angle and, quite possibly, resolved. It is a change of mood or direction, however slight. The turn is as important to the sonnet as is the fact that there are fourteen lines, each of ten syllables, each written primarily in iambs.

In an Italian sonnet, the turn comes at the beginning of the octave; in the Shakespearean sonnet, it occurs at the beginning of the thirteenth line. In both cases, it opens the problem already set out for solution and begins to ease the load built up in the first eight or twelve lines.

THE CLOSE

A sonnet closes with either a sestet or a couplet. If you are writing an Italian sonnet, you will have six lines to unwind and present your resolution. That is enough time to make a reasonable argument, to apply some logic, and to think through the outcome.

In the Shakespearean sonnet, you have only two lines, which must rhyme with each other, to get out of the dilemma or situation you've spent twelve lines detailing. As a result, these sonnets are more likely to be resolved through wit, through a flash of insight (often presented as a strong visual image), or through irony.

BUILDING THE SONNET

Let's say you've been assigned the task of writing a sonnet. How would you begin? Start by reading a number of sonnets in different forms, to see if that gives you any ideas.

Or start by thinking of a subject about which you'd like to write a sonnet. It might help to know that sonnets, traditionally, have been written about love.

If you already have a subject, you could try free writing on it for several sessions. You could write three pages longhand each morning for a week, then comb through the pages for language that you find intriguing. Then pull out lines and begin to shape them to ten syllables each, in iambic pentameter, with the sonnet rhyme scheme of your choice.

Some students, pressed for time, find that writing one ten syllable line in rough iambic pentameter that ends with a common rhyming sound is a good beginning. A second line gives them a second rhyme sound, and they're off, fitting their syllables into the pattern of unaccented, accented, ten syllables to a line, the rhyme scheme pushing them on.

Some poets play a game called *lightning sonnets*, in which the rhyme scheme is made up first, sometimes with words being chosen at random from whatever books lie at hand. Next, each poet in a group writes a sonnet to fit that rhyme scheme. It's somewhat like dealing everyone the same bridge hand and seeing how many ways, and how well, it can be played.

Sense is not often the strong point of sonnets written in either fashion; however, teachers who assign the writing of sonnets on strict deadlines and expect sense are perhaps asking a bit much. Just work on the pattern, getting the syllables and accent correct, perfecting your rhyme scheme, and so on.

Try writing several sonnets to see whether the process gets easier. Warning: Sonnet writing can be addictive. There are some people who can't write just one.

WRITING A VILLANELLE

Suppose you've been asked to write a villanelle. First, find out what a villanelle is. Originally, it was an Italian country song or dance. In the sixteenth century, it became a French verse form, that was taken up by poets writing in English in the nineteenth century.

For a time, villanelles were used for writing light verse, but they have since been written by some of the best poets of our time. Dylan Thomas's villanelle "Do Not Go Gentle" is addressed to his dying father and resonates with both grief and rage.

Find a villanelle and study its pattern. The plan of a villanelle is relatively easy to deduce. The lines are not metered so much as counted; you need to have the same number of syllables in each line, but the lines may be of any length.

Nineteen lines are divided into six stanzas—five triplets and one quatrain. They turn on two rhymes and the poem is built on two refrains. The refrains are lines one and three, complete. Line one reappears as lines six, twelve, and eighteen; line three reappears as lines nine, fifteen, and nineteen, finishing the poem.

The blueprint of the villanelle looks like this:

VILLANELLE

A^1
b
A^2

a
b
A^1

a
b
A^2

a
b
A^1

a
b
A^2

a
b
A¹
A²

Example of a villanelle from *Villanelles for Mother Goose*:

When land is gone and money spent
Fair weather friends leave you alone.
Then learning is most excellent.

You know you cannot pay the rent.
All out of meat you gnaw the bone.
When land is gone and money spent,

The rich will urge you to repent:
You are reaping as you've sown.
Then learning is most excellent.

Although you've not a single cent,
Keats and Yeats are still your own.
When land is gone and money spent

You will still know what Plato meant.
Although it can't repay a loan,
your learning is most excellent.

Whatever wisdom you've been sent
Stays on when all your credit's blown.
When land is gone and mony spent,
then learning is most excellent.

To write a good villanelle, choose with care your refrains, which will serve as your first and third lines as well as repeating end lines. Make sure they have resonance and are memorable in some way. It's great if their meaning seems to spread out from them like ripples from a stone thrown into a pool.

Of course, the lines should also be musical. And you must remember to choose rhyme words that are easily matched in English.

In one of her early attempts to write a villanelle, called "The Aviary," Elizabeth Bishop was daunted by a number of factors. Not the least of these, one suspects, was her rhyme scheme, which included words such as: *fiduciary, subsidiary, sumptuary,* and *beneficiary.* Even a master of the craft of poetry such as Bishop couldn't handle the complexity of these rhymes.

In looking at her successful villanelle "One Art," you'll see that here again, she chose challenging rhyme words, including *master, disaster, content, intent,* and *continent.* Other successful villanelles tend to use simpler sounds; such as *day* and *light,* in Dylan Thomas's famous villanelle.

THE BIRTH OF A VILLANELLE

In speaking about the composition of her villanelle, "One Art," Bishop claimed it was a gift, that writing it was as easy as writing a letter.

In truth, she wrote at least seventeen drafts of the poem. A brief look at her process may encourage you to keep trying with your villanelle.

First, Bishop began with notes, written in a kind of free association, that are an unedited catalog of losses. In the margins of this draft, and in the next draft, she begins to set up a rhyme scheme: *ever/never/forever; geography/scenery; intelligent/ continent/sent/spent/lent.*

By the second draft, the poem is clearly an incomplete villanelle. The "art of losing isn't hard to master" is by now the first line, and the third line ends with *no disaster.* The final stanza in this draft is crossed out.

It was not unusual for Elizabeth Bishop to invest years in the composition of her verse.

In the next several drafts, she edits the catalog of losses, and sets the rhyme scheme firmly. The fifth draft is a simple list of end rhymes, but the last stanza is a problem.

Each version of the poem distances the pain a little more, depersonalizing it, and moving it away from confession, toward art. She struggles with the last stanza through the rest of the drafts, until she finally gets it right. Here, then, is the product of all her work. Doesn't she make it look easy?

ONE ART

Elizabeth Bishop

The art of losing isn't hard to master;
so many things seem filled with the intent
to be lost that their loss is no disaster.

Lose something everyday. Accept the fluster
of lost door keys, the hour badly spent.
The art of losing isn't hard to master.

Then practice losing farther, losing faster:
places, and names, and where it was you meant
to travel. None of these will bring disaster.

I lost my mother's watch. And look! my last, or
next-to-last, of three loved houses went.
The art of losing isn't hard to master.

I lost two cities, lovely ones. And, vaster,
some realms I owned, two rivers, a continent.
I miss them, but it wasn't a disaster.

—Even losing you (the joking voice, a gesture
I love) I shan't have lied. It's evident
the art of losing's not too hard to master
though it may look like (Write it!) like disaster.

Notice how the villanelle works with two opposing ideas, and how many sets of two's there are in the poem:

130

two rivers, two cities, and so on. Duality seems to play an important role in writing a convincing villanelle.

YOUR VILLANELLE

Try beginning your villanelle by choosing a couplet that appeals to you. Look at Mother Goose rhymes, advertising, and books of poetry for material on which to build. For instance, you could write a villanelle based on the rhyme:

> *When land is gone and money spent,*
> *then learning is most excellent.*

Fit the refrains into the blueprint where they belong and write the connecting tissue.

If you're starting from scratch, it's a good idea to have one or both of your lines begin with a verb, as Thomas does:

> *Do not go gentle into that good night,*
> *Old age should burn and rave at close of day:*
> *Rage, rage against the dying of the light.*

Use simple words and diction. And, at least for the first few attempts, stick with rhyme sounds that have lots of possibilities in English. You could even borrow someone else's rhyme scheme and write your own villanelle.

SESTINAS

Like the villanelle, the sestina form comes from the French.

Sestinas tend to be more narrative than sonnets or villanelles. Because of their length, they make great vehicles for telling stories. You can think of them as conversations in which certain words keep being repeated, used in new ways, or varied.

The lines of a sestina can be of any length, and there is no rhyme involved. Rather, there is repetition of another sort. The sestina has six six-line stanzas and a final three-line stanza called the envoy. Below is a blueprint for a sestina. Note that the capital letters don't refer to rhymes, but to the end words that are repeated every time the corresponding letter reappears.

SESTINA

A
B
C
D
E
F

F
A
E
B
D
C

C
F
D
A
B
E

E
C
B
F
A
D

D
E
A
C
F
B

B
D
F
E
C
A

B...E
D...C
F...A

Example of a Sestina:

The Long Winter

The long winter of terror and cliché
has ended. It is March. Crocuses
swell in the garden, purple, yellow, white.
At home, though I haven't been there,
laundry hangs in the sun and the wind
slaps wet sheets into expected freshness.

The sheets dry. Their freshness,
like these immaculate days, is cliché,
and the March wind is no younger than
      the wind
that delivers our blizzards all winter.
      Those crocuses
seen newborn, but I have seen them there,
blooming like years, before, the white

ones no more pure than snow which lay, white
all winter in the arms of trees. Their freshness
delights you, and you smile, and say, "There.
It is spring. Our kisses are not cliché.
And your terror was only the sound of the wind,
ruffling the petals of the crocuses—"

And your kisses bloom in my mouth
    like crocuses,
pure, passionate, the purple, the white,
and you lie in my arms like the wind.
I think toward summer. Will this freshness
mellow and bear fruit, or wither to cliché
as I to wife, and run to seed? There

are no answers to these questions you say.
There are the sheets flapping in the sun,
    the crocuses
dropping like their petals like cliché
into the conservation of the garden, the white
roses budding early, the freshness
of jays coasting on wind.

And you and I, listening to the wind,
and you, whispering, "There. There."
Winter will come again, our kisses lose
    their freshness,
and love unpetal like crocuses,
the purple, the yellow, yes, even the white.
And our kisses will dwindle to cliché.

But kiss me now. The freshness of crocuses
eases my terror of the wind, of winter waiting
    there, white
and unending, behind this brief sweet season
    of cliché.

As you can see, the end words are repeated again and again. After the first stanza, they appear in a regular pattern: the last word of the sixth line becomes the last word of the first line in the next stanza. The last word of the first line of the first stanza becomes the last word of the second line of the next stanza. The crisscrossing continues, until all the end words have appeared in each position in each stanza.

The final three-line envoy uses the six end words, too—two in each line, one in the middle and one at the end. Although the sestina form requires that the words in the envoy be used in a particular order, you can really use any order within the envoy that works for you.

WRITING YOUR SESTINA

When writing a sestina, choose your end words with care. You are going to use them seven times in the poem. You want them to be words that offer you some flexibility—words that have more than one meaning, such as *rose*, or words that can be used as both a noun and a verb, such as *fly*. It's fun to include one word that is something of a challenge, as well. You might use one adjective that can also double as a noun.

There are several difficult things about a sestina. For one, you have to use the same end word to (1) end a stanza, (2) as the last word of the next line, and (3) as the first line of the next stanza. Because there is so much repetition in the sestina, you might find it makes sense to avoid other repetitions within the poem.

Words with multiple meanings, called homonyms, work well in sestinas. These words sound alike, but are spelled differently: *red/read, two/to/too,* and *heart/hart.*

Try using mostly nouns and verbs as end words, along with an adjective or two. Limit using prepositions or conjunctions as end words—they are tricky to repeat.

OTHER FORMS

There are many forms for poems that have not been discussed here. In general, however, if you want to write in a given form, find a map of the form—consult a good poetry text, such as *Western Wind*, or a book about forms, such as *Teachers and Writers Book of Forms*, or *The Book of Forms* by Lewis Turco.

Find several poems written in the form that interests you. (See *Strong Measures: Contemporary American Poetry in Traditional Forms*, Harper and Row, 1986, edited by Philip Dacey & David Jauss.)

What kind of content does the form handle well, or badly? For instance, limericks always seem to be joking, ironic, and perhaps a bit off-color by their very nature. Don't let this discourage you—if you want to write a funereal limerick, give it a try. If you accomplish it, you'll have something to be really proud of; but even if you don't, you'll learn a lot along the way.

Once you have the pattern and some samples, see if you can analyze what works. You'll notice that many villanelles use Dylan Thomas's technique of beginning lines with verbs—which means you can make the verb imperative or, by ending the previous line with a subject, you can make the verb indicative. You can even make the verb interrogative (asking a question).

When you have a sense of the form, choose a subject and begin to write. Or simply begin to write in the form. If you are writing a sestina, you can pick six words at random and jump right in. You might also look through some of your old drafts, see if anything looks as if it wants to be coaxed into form.

Writing in form is like doing scales at the piano, practicing figures on ice, or doing barre work in ballet. It's a way to loosen up, to practice, to refine fundamental techniques of the art in which you're working. Like meditation, it is a form of discipline. No one does figures as part of an ice-skating routine, yet figures teach discipline, balance, and control.

Writing in forms will help you gain control of your voice, your talent, the language, and the techniques of poetry.

FREE VERSE

Free verse has no set meter; the lines are rhythmic and vary in length. Free verse is generally unrhymed. It is built on grammatical structures and often held together by repetition.

Consider the following poem by Philip Booth:

WORDS

Tears. Tears after all.
I lean over her: I know.
I know how you feel.

I lie. It's true:
she's bleeding. She's
readying herself for

dying. Or birth. She's
a child, her own daughter,
the mother she's lost.

She's better. Eased.
I say her her name.
I want to cry. I want

to speak what tears can't.
Emptied, her eyes
reach for mine.

Notice how the poem is built on repetitions of words ("Tears. Tear after all" or "I know, / I know how you feel") as well as repetitions of grammatical forms: "She's a child," "she's lost," "she's better."

Free verse has both its enemies and its champions. Robert Frost compared writing poetry in free verse to playing tennis without a net. Yet other poets, such as Allen Ginsberg, want the poem to suggest its own form and want to enhance form, rather than impose it on the subject at hand.

In an individual poem, you need to choose between formal strategies and free verse. But in general, there's no need to stick to one or the other. Try both, and see which is more congenial to your muse.

The Line

In general, the unit of free verse composition is the line. The line is an aid in composing, and the lines of any given poem can all be short, all long, or of varied lengths.

Poets seem to have a sixth sense about what works best for them and for their material. Some, like Philip Booth, write primarily in short lines. Others, like Allen Ginsberg and Walt Whitman, write primarily in long lines. Richard Wright and other poets use a combination of line lengths, all within a single poem.

MARY BLY

Richard Wright

*I sit here, doing nothing, alone, worn out by
    long winter.
I feel the light breath of the newborn child.
Her face is smooth as the side of an apricot.
Eyes quick as her blonde mother's hands.*

She has full, soft, red hair, and as she
  lies quiet
In her tall mother's arms, her delicate hands
Weave back and forth.
I feel the seasons changing beneath me,
Under the floor.
She is braiding the waters of air into the
  plaited manes of happy colts.
They canter, without making a sound, along
  the shores
Of melting snow.

Here again, notice how the poem is built through repetition of words: "Her blond mother's hands.... her tall mother's arms..." and grammatical structures: "I sit, I feel, I feel..."

Another technique used in writing free verse is called *open field*, which involves putting together short, medium, and long lines, chunks of prose, freely indenting, and using blank space expressively. In short, it means arranging the words on the page so that they best convey your poetic message.

Robert Duncan practices this free verse form. He coined the phrase *open field*, and it is similar to Charles Olson's *projective verse*.

Line Breaks

The line is the main controlling unit of free verse. But how do you know when you have come to the end of one line and are ready to begin the next?

There are several places that make sense as line endings. You might stop your lines at the end of the sentence, as in the first four lines of the Wright poem above. You might also break the lines at natural pauses: after a comma, say, or between phrases.

Try breaking the line in the middle of a phrase, as Philip Booth does above. This will give you a feeling

Poet Richard Wright works in his study.

that you are cutting across the grain of the poem. It introduces a kind of counterpoint, as the sense of the sentence and the end of the line do not correspond, disrupting the ordinary forms of syntax. You can break a line at a point of suspense, as Booth does in his line "readying herself for."

Wherever you break your lines, the poem must be both rhythmic and musical—even if it is not metered. Free verse is free of meter, but it still has rhythm. The rhythm is irregular, but like some jazz rhythms, it is still there.

Don't think that because it's free verse it can be dull and flat. It can't. Dull and flat aren't free—they're boring.

To enliven your free verse, vary the ways in which your lines end. You should end stop lines, coming to a full syntactical stop at the end of the line. In other lines, let the sense run past the line ending onto the next line. This practice is called *enjambment*, and it can help to keep a free-verse poem moving and lively.

Word Choices

Because free verse is closely aligned to speech, you'll want, for the most part, to use fairly simple, concrete words.

Consider what poet Louise Glück, a master of free verse, has written on this subject:

What fascinated me were the possibilities of context. What I responded to, on the page, was the way a poem could liberate, by means of a word's setting, through subtleties of timing, of pacing, that word's full and surprising range of meaning. It seemed to me that simple language suited this enterprise.

The Sound of Free Verse

From the examples quoted above, and from your own reading of poetry, you may have noticed that free verse sounds quite different from metered verse. For one thing, there isn't that insistent meter urging you on, the way the beat of a song drives you forward. Free verse is more like speech than song, and it's often quite meditative.

Free verse uses the music of everyday words and everyday speech patterns but heightens them, accentuating them so that we can really hear the music within the language we use every day.

Writing in Free Verse

Free verse writing theory is both hard to come by and difficult to put into practice. For example, if a breath is the measure of line length, as Allen Ginsberg claims, would that mean you can only write short lines after climbing twelve flights of stairs?

The best way to learn to write free verse is to find a poet whose free verse you like and admire. By imitating, studying, and copying that poet's style, you will teach yourself how to write free verse.

TEN

WHO'S VOICE IS IT ANYWAY?

I experience, as a reader, two primary modes of poetic speech. One, to the reader, feels like confidence, one seems interrupted meditation.
—Louise Glück

I want to hear you, not your voice.
—voice teacher's maxim

If you read a number of poems written in the same form—villanelles, sonnets, sestinas—by various poets, one of the most interesting differences you will note is the difference of voice.

In Dylan Thomas's villanelle, for instance, we hear an angry, raging voice. Elizabeth Bishop's voice is milder, self-mocking, ironic. She claims that the art of losing isn't hard to master, but she means exactly the opposite. And in Theodore Roethke's villanelle, which begins, "I wake to sleep and take my waking slow," we hear a soft, melodic voice; a voice that sounds barely awake. Three different poets, writing in the same form, in three different voices.

DIALOGUE

One way that poets try different voices is by writing dialogue, conversations between two characters. Using dialogue can create a lively give and take, allowing for contradictions, interruptions, and a wide variety of tone that would be hard to accomplish when using only a single speaker.

If you'd like to see how dialogue can be used well in poems, look at the work of Robert Frost, who often uses dialogue and direct quotation in his early poems. Sometimes he uses two present speakers, and a third, off-stage as it were, who is quoted. Frost's poem "Death of the Hired Man" makes brilliant use of this technique.

When Frost does not use two voices directly, he sometimes quotes another speaker within the poem, conveying a sense of two voices. In "Mending Wall," for example, the speaker quotes his neighbor as saying, "Good fences make good neighbors." The poem is mostly a one-sided argument between the speaker and the neighbor, who merely repeats what he hears. Dialogues give the poet an efficient way to present conflict, clashes, and severe differences of opinion.

VOICE

Every poem has a voice; that is, we assume that every poem is being spoken (or sung) by someone. It's very important that this voice seem real, not invented or artificial.

Wallace Stevens's speakers use extraordinary and ornate diction and deal frequently in abstraction. Yet his lines always feel as if they are coming from a real human being. Look at his poem, "The Emperor of Ice Cream," and listen carefully to the speaker's voice.

It's fantastic, yet completely authoritative—a convincingly human voice—we hear in this poem. Voice is the way poets draw on themselves as they write.

HEARING VOICES

Reread a few of the poems you really like and listen to the voice of the person speaking. Can you describe this person? What do you know about him, her, or them?

Does the voice confide in you? Is it meditative, thinking something over? Does the voice sing, scream, or urge to action? Is the voice seductive?

It's possible for a voice in a poem to do any— maybe all—of these things. See if you can find poems that have a range of tones of voice.

YOUR VOICE

Every writer has a natural voice. That voice can be polished in writing. Your voice is the way you write when you don't have time to be charming, when you're really carried away by what you have to say.

Your voice includes the words you choose, the pauses in your breathing, as well as the rate at which you speak: briskly, slowly, angrily, rapidly.

You are most likely to write in your own voice when you write about things that matter to you. Although voice is an important component of poetry, there is no formula for finding it, only hints, suggestions, and clues.

TONE AND VOICE

Voice has a great deal of influence on tone, and vice versa. Tone is, after all, affected by word choice. It makes a difference in tone whether you say *wife*, *bride*, *partner*, or *spouse*. Some word choices are warmer and friendlier than others.

The length of your sentences also affects your tone. Short sentences sting. Long flowing sentences can convey a sense of leisure and graciousness.

Phrasing is an element of tone, too. Whether you say "Swiftly in the nights," "Nights, swiftly," or "Swiftly at night" can make a subtle difference.

Rhythms are another dimension. Rapid, tripping rhythms convey a different tone from slow, heavy, ponderous ones.

In addition to all these factors, voice and tone are also affected by the speaker's attitude toward himself or herself, toward the audience, and toward the subject of the poem. All these factors—sentence length, phrasing, rhythm, and speaker attitude—influence word choice, pitch, and modulation and create a poem's tone.

You might, in fact, think of tone as an aspect of voice, as in "tone of voice." We've all heard someone make an innocent sounding remark in a tone of voice that renders it unacceptable. And every child has been scolded by a parent: "Don't take that tone with me."

Sarcasm is usually a tone. Irony is a tone. Anger has a tone. All these elements can affect the quality of your voice.

DRAMATIC MONOLOGUE

Within a single body of work, poets can use several different voices. Some poets do this by assuming the role of the character who is speaking in the poem and writing what is called a *dramatic monologue*.

In "My Last Duchess," for example, Robert Browning becomes the speaker, who is, one hopes, very different from the poet. Browning assumes the voice of a Renaissance duke who has murdered his last wife.

In his collection of dramatic monologues called *Empires*, poet Richard Moore tries on a range of voices, including those of Aaron Burr, Jay Gould, Archimedes, and Cleopatra. In "Crusoe in England," Elizabeth Bishop speaks with the voice of Robinson Crusoe, back in his native land, thinking about all those years he spent on a desert island. And even Emily Dickinson, who never took on an obvious persona, claimed in letters that the speaker of her poems was not herself but a "supposed person."

In dramatic monologue, the voice one assumes is called a *persona*, or mask. By assuming this persona, the poet makes it clear that the person speaking the poem is not identical to the person writing it. The author, in effect, counterfeits the speech of another person in a particular situation. And while it is true that the speaker's voice often carries the ring of the author's own voice, it's also true that speaking as another can free us to speak more truly and more truthfully.

WRITING A DRAMATIC MONOLOGUE

Try this exercise: assemble a collection of photos of people you don't know. Look in the library for a book of photos. You could use work by Dorothea Lange, Diane Arbus, or André Kertész. You could also work from a collection of paintings or postcards of people who interest you. Or buy old photos of people you know nothing about from a secondhand store.

If you have no objection to handling tarot cards, you might also use a deck of these for this exercise. The Ryder-Waite deck, in which every card carries an illustration, is widely available and makes a good deck for this purpose.

Once you have assembled your group of pictures, select two at random. Then write a poem about one, or both, of the pictures in this way:

Pretend that you are within the picture you have chosen. You are one of those photographed or painted. If you are using tarot cards, you can be any of the people in the card.

Now, speak from that person's point of view, adopting his or her persona. If you are writing about a photo of a girl in a swing, speak to the audience from her point of view. Tell us what you are wearing, what you are doing, what you can see from where you are, where you are coming from, where you are going, what has just happened or is about to happen.

Be sure to include many of the physical details from within the picture. If, as you're writing, other things occur to you, write them down. If the character begins to tell a story, let it go. See what happens. Allow your speakers to reveal themselves in speech.

At the very end of the poem, take a leap: tell us some secret of the person for whom you are speaking. You will have to make this up. The answer is not in the picture but somewhere inside of you. Don't write down, "My secret is that I have no secret," or "If I tell you it won't be a secret." The whole point is to let your imagination provide you with information. There is no right or wrong—it's just practice.

When you've finished, put the poem aside for a few days and let it breathe. Then look at it again. You should notice many concrete details and hear the voice of a person rooted in a place, a time, a moment, a costume—someone caught in the act. See if, with a little revision, additional writing, or editing, you can make what you've written into a poem.

The beauty of this exercise is that it forces you to take a point of view, to tell a story from inside a person standing in a particular place. Point of view, an important aspect of storytelling, is vital in narratives, including narrative poems.

Point of view is also important in the lyric poem. Many lyric poets root their work in the real, in the solid. Because we know that Keats is listening in the fragrant dark to his nightingale, for example, we are easily able to imagine the scene and the feelings he is writing about.

WRITING FROM LIFE

When you write from a picture, you tell the story and you are part of the story you are telling. The picture simplifies the elements; that is, they've already been edited and arranged by someone else.

When you turn to your life, it's a little harder to sort out what should and should not be included in the poem. The photo from which you worked might have featured a family of the last century standing on a screen porch. The picture tells you what to include, and what you don't see is left out. You can accomplish the same thing by making sure you picture yourself in a particular place, at a particular time, looking at particular things. If you were a camera, what aspects of the scene would you be able to record?

Now write another poem, based on a picture of yourself, using the above technique. Root your poem, grounding it in the obvious details. But this time, tell us more. Tell us the secret of the picture—the mysterious, invisible thing that only you know.

CONFESSIONAL POETRY

Some poets—going all the way back to Catullus, who wrote in ancient Rome—assert that they are not their poems. Or as a translation of a Catullus poem put it:

> *You miss the point—my poetry*
> *is simply not the same as me.*
>
> (Ormsby Myers)

Other poets insist on the relationship between their poetic and personal voices. During the 1960s, for instance, in reaction against academic, ironic poems stuffed with multiple meanings or ambiguities, some poets began to write what has come to be known as *confessional poetry.*

In general, in a confessional poem, the speaker and the poet are assumed to be one. There is no space between the persona and the poet.

Of course, this is not and cannot be completely true, for an entire person cannot get on the page. But poetry that makes this assumption can be alarmingly immediate, and edgy. Read some of the poems of Robert Lowell, the work of W. D. Snodgrass, or poems by Anne Sexton or Sylvia Plath to get a feel for confessional poetry.

Perhaps you will find it easier to write a confessional poem than to work with the distance that a persona provides.

THE HONEST VOICE

Some poets like to assume an artificial voice when they write. Others try to tell it all, in their own voices. Honesty in poetry is valued by many, but particularly by Allen Ginsberg and the Beat poets.

Ginsberg put it this way in an interview, "The problem is...when you approach your muse...to talk as frankly as you would talk with yourself or with your friends," and later comments that it's important to be

150

able "to commit to writing, to write, the same way that you…are!"

This quality of voice is evident in Ginsberg's poems. He comes through as a real person, a genuine voice talking about his own life.

You might enjoy writing a poem in which you speak as yourself to someone very close to you: a best friend, a sister or brother, a favorite teacher. Or try to imagine yourself telling the truth about something very important to a total stranger, someone with whom you feel rapport but whom you will never see again. Don't worry about fancy language, rhythm, and so forth. Really work at revealing something hidden about yourself, and something important to you. Your subject can be anything: that you are disturbed by the color of your skin, that you are secretly very fond of your big ears, the way a particular moment felt, or some terrible or wonderful experience.

FREEWRITING AGAIN

Freewriting is a way to get to know your natural voice. Let yourself write for up to twenty minutes at a time. Each day put the pages away in an envelope in a desk drawer. After a week of writing, reread what you have done. Underline places where your voice seems most authentic to you. Retype those sections and see if you can arrange them into a poem.

Or, try writing a poem using only objects you can see from where you are sitting. Be inventive. Have objects do different things. Elizabeth Bishop uses this technique in a marvelous poem called "11 O'clock News."

Another way to try to find your voice is to write a poem in answer to a question. Keep a list of questions you hear or read. Keep a journal. Take several unrelated journal entries and weave them into a single poem.

In your search for your own voice, you might find it helpful to try on the voices of other writers. Many of us do this unconsciously; we write as if we were the people whose poetry we love. There is some danger in doing this, but not much. You might enjoy making your imitations conscious, trying to adopt the voice of another the way a comedienne does impressions.

You could also write the same poetic material in different voices. Write a poem about a flower, for instance, as if you were Emily Dickinson, Anne Sexton, and Adrienne Rich.

ANOTHER VOICE TO TRY

Many people have an inner critic who appears when they begin to write. This critic usually says things such as, "*While* isn't spelled like that," "You can't really write," "This is a boring beginning," and so on. As an exercise, try writing with the voice of this inner critic. Let him or her star in the poem, give them a say, let them take as long as he or she likes. Usually, these critics don't produce very interesting stories or poems, but you never know. It could be fun to let them speak their piece.

Whatever you do, though, don't write as an imposter, using someone else's voice. You have many voices, and you should try to learn and use them all. All you ever really have to work with is the quality of your own presence. Writing is always revealing. Even when we adopt the stance of another person in a poem, we reveal ourselves. And when we think we are being most open and revelatory about ourselves, we often hide more than we reveal.

Of course, what we choose to hide is a kind of revelation in itself. When someone calls to say he or she is planning to stop by, what do you clean up or put away so he or she won't see it? The answer could provide you with the beginning of a poem.

REVISION

Look back at the poem you've drafted. What can you say about the voice you hear as you read it? Do you like the voice? Is it yours, or someone else's? Make any changes—in word choice, rhythm, sentence length, or phrasing that will move the voice toward the one you want to hear.

ELEVEN

DISTILLATION AND FINISHING

Poetry is life distilled.
—Gwendolyn Brooks

Poetry is an act of distillation.
—Diane Ackerman

Distillation, used in a literal sense, involves a change of state. For instance, when a liquid is distilled, it's converted into a gas. Later, through condensation, the gas will return to liquid. Meanwhile, some part of the original substance is separated out and purified. Distillation makes it possible to get to the essence of the thing distilled.

Distillation was probably first used in the production of intoxicating beverages. Today, it is employed in the creation of many products, from petroleum derivatives to perfume.

DISTILLING POETRY

When you distill a poem, you might change its state— from language that's close to prose to something approaching poetry. More than that, when you distill a poem, you purify it, extracting the essence of your experience. The challenge is always to capture that essence in the fewest possible words.

Some writers talk about this process as revision, or editing, or paring down. Still others call it compression. Putting editorial and critical pressure on the language, they make their poems more dense, more compact. Not surprisingly, a poem that's been properly compressed and distilled tends to take up less space on the page.

When you have created what you believe to be your final draft, let it rest for a while, then look at it closely. See if you can compress, tighten, or concentrate what's left. If you can, your poem has a better chance of making a strong impression on your reader.

LESS IS MORE

"Less is more," the great designers and architects say, and in poetry, it is often so. Think of Michelangelo, who "saw" the statue inside the marble and liberated it by cutting away everything that was not the statue. You want to take anything extra, anything distracting, away.

Film and video producers and directors face this same challenge. They usually shoot several times more footage than is required for a picture. Consequently, what happens in the editing room—what gets left in, what gets left out, and in what order—is a vital step in the process of creation. There is art in removing excess.

TALKING IT THROUGH

What you leave in and what you take out will determine what your poem finally says. If you're not quite sure what you're trying to say, making these choices will be difficult, if not impossible.

One way to determine what you are trying to say is to write or talk it out. Sit down and write, "This poem is really about..." and fill in the blank with as few words as possible. State the gist of the poem. Then look at your draft again and take out anything that doesn't contribute to that idea.

Better still, sit down with a friend and get some help. Let your friend read the poem, then ask what he or she thinks it's about. If your friend gets it, great! Ask if there seems to be anything extra in the poem, anything you can remove. Really listen to what he or she says. Make notes.

If your reader doesn't get the point, state it. Tell her: "This poem is really about..." and state the point as simply as you can. It's a good idea to have a tape recorder running when you say this part. You will probably say a few things you'll want to capture for your poem.

You could also ask your friend to take notes of what you say. Many times, the words people say about their poems aren't in the poems at all. And by adding—or substituting—at least some of what you've said out loud, you can sharpen and tighten your poem.

CLEANING THE FISH

"When you clean a fish, the first thing that goes is the head," wrote Kenneth Atchity in *A Writer's Time*, "generally, manuscripts should receive the same treatment." Look at the beginning of your poem and see if it starts with words, sentences, perhaps an entire stanza that sets up the poem for you, the writer, but in fact delays the reader from getting to the core of the poem.

Try your poem without the opening line, without the first few lines. Is there a better opening hiding halfway down the first stanza? Then begin there. Later in the poem, you may need to incorporate some of the information you've cut out. You may not.

Likewise, take a look at the end of the poem. Writers sometimes end a piece of writing several times before they let it go. See if your poem really ends a few lines, or perhaps a stanza, earlier. Can you drop the last line or the last few lines and come away with a stronger poem?

Again, it may be necessary to take some of the words you cut from the end of your poem and build them back elsewhere in the poem for clarity. If that's the case, do it.

REMOVING MODIFIERS

Extra words are like scaffolding. You need scaffolding to help you build a house, but once the house is up, the scaffolding comes down. You probably needed extra words to help you create or build your poem. But once the poem is done, or nearly done, you must search out the scaffolding and take it down. Then you'll be able to see—and make the best of—what's left.

Begin by removing all modifiers—all adjectives and adverbs. That's right—*all* modifiers. Just cross them out.

Read through what's left, and see if it isn't tighter, clearer, easier to understand what you're talking about.

If you find a place where you absolutely must have a modifier, put it back in.

If you keep some adjectives, make sure they're working hard. Don't just repeat the same meaning in different words: *important, meaningful, momentous*. Rather, use each new adjective to turn the meaning somewhat. Use adjectives to add a new dimension: *important, translucent, odd.*

Removing modifiers can be an easy exercise if you've written a poem in free verse. If, however, you've written in a formal metrical pattern—whether it's unrhymed iambic pentameter or the Italian sonnet—making these deletions will be more difficult. That's because poets who write in form are often tempted to pad out the meter of a line with empty syllables.

Fortunately, these are easy to find. Look for such words as *very, really, nice, big, small,* and so on. Do you really need to say *white* when you're talking about snow or *black* when you're describing ebony? Have you added *lovely* or *beautifully*—words that don't help us see or add to the meaning? If so, grit your teeth. Grab a pencil. Cross them out.

When you remove these words you'll have holes in your poem. You have two choices. You can work hard to revise the poem, including only words that actually advance the action and don't just pad out the meter. This can be excellent practice; it will push you toward discovering new things you didn't even know you wanted to say.

Or you could decide to let the poem stand as is, abandoning the formal structure and letting the feeling you've captured stand alone. Of course, if you're writing an Italian sonnet on assignment for a class, the teacher might prefer to see the padded version. She may want to see that you really understand the form, even if what you've written doesn't rival Petrarch.

Why not submit both the padded version and the leaner model? It could stimulate some interesting class discussion, or at least begin a dialogue within yourself, about the relative importance of form and content. (In the end, in poetry, they are equally important.)

If you can't find the syllables you need to make a perfect sonnet, don't despair. Many poems that don't fit the sonnet form exactly are considered sonnets. There's the work of Robert Lowell, whose fourteen line poems don't necessarily rhyme and usually aren't written in iambic pentameter, but are called sonnets, anyway. There are poems of fourteen lines, rhyming in the sonnet pattern, in which each line is a single word, and these are called sonnets, too. Perhaps the best-known pared-down sonnet is the one by Elizabeth Bishop:

SONNET

Caught—the bubble
in the spirit-level,
a creature divided;
and the compass needle
wobbling and wavering,
undecided.
Freed—the broken
thermometer's mercury
running away:
and the rainbow-bird
from the narrow bevel
of the empty mirror,
flying wherever
it feels like, gay!

CONCENTRATING

Good chefs create rich stocks, concentrating flavorful liquids by long simmering. Although you shouldn't literally leave your poem over a low heat for a long time, there's often something to be said for letting your poem simmer, metaphorically.

Put your draft away for some time, as long as you feel is proper. That could be overnight, a week, or a few weeks. The Roman poet Horace suggested putting your work away for nine years—but this might be a bit long if you have to hand something in! Think of this as putting the poem on a back burner. Tuck it into your unconscious mind, and let it cook.

When you look at it again, see if can find more ways to compress it. Perhaps you have said essentially the same thing twice, in different words. Delete one or the other or combine the best parts of each into a single statement.

Maybe you've added detail that isn't strictly needed. It may be very interesting, but if it derails or waylays the reader's attention, cut it out. You don't want your reader worrying about things that aren't essential to your poem. It may be hard to part with this material. Save it, if you wish, for another poem. Copy it into a notebook or a computer file. But be brave. Cut. It will only strengthen your poem.

Consider the following draft of the opening stanza of a poem.

AGAINST ROMANCE

The moon has rebuilt the boats below
  the water,
replicas of cabin cruisers, outboards,
  dinghies,
in meticulous detail with her pale light.
Now she recreates herself, floating on
  the surface
as the tide laps out down river, revealing
mud flats studded with dull stones.
The wind lifts salt smells, first perfume
  of apples
fallen in abandoned orchards, a flight
  from death
to death, crabbed branches into long
  brown grass.

Notice how much space and time the poet spends discussing and detailing the boats in the river. Unfortunately, the poem isn't about the boats, and these details are a distraction—however momentary—to the reader. You really can't afford to lose your reader's attention for a second. So it would probably be best to trim these lines.

After time and thought, the poet rewrote the stanza, compressing and strengthening it. The specific details of the boats are gone, along with other details. What remains is more concentrated and focuses the reader on the main issue under discussion. The reader has less opportunity to go astray.

AGAINST ROMANCE

The moon has rebuilt the boats below
   the water
and now recreates herself, floating
as the tide laps out over mud flats. The wind
lifts salt smells, first perfume of fallen apples.

A POEM IN PROGRESS

Theory is one thing; practice is another. Let's take a look at a poem in progress and then at the final product.

The poem below had been worked on for some time. An early draft ran nearly twenty pages, typed double spaced. Finally, the poet had trimmed it to two pages and finally to fewer than twenty-five lines.

BERNINI: BACCHANAL; FAUN BEING
TEASED BY CHILDREN

A naked marble faun besieged by twins.
Each step around reveals a different view:
cheek to stone cheek, shoulder, elbow,

apples, plums, the faun's hand
grasping the rigid branch.
A child's bottom not quite astride
a hound's lean back.
A lion's pelt flung across the trunk.
A lizard suns where everlastings bloom.
I pace the pavanne Bernini planned.
I become the marble in his hand.
And I have seen these marble boys before,
cherubs napping in far galleries.
Slack-bellied, bronze, or grouped around
    a tomb,
they wear the same mischief on their lips,
the same hint of their power to undo.
I've seen this same three-quarter faun in you.
The dog reaches up as the grapes
    drape down.
The boys and faun carouse eternally.
My daughter lengthens into girl
and rounds toward wife.
I lose my little beauty by the hour.
I'm past the telling moment of my life.
The marble faun ascends the marble tree.

Time passed, and the poet showed the draft to several colleagues. She thought about the work and revised it again. The final poem looks, and sounds, like this:

BERNINI: BACCHANAL; FAUN BEING
TEASED BY CHILDREN

A naked marble faun besieged by twins.
  Cheek to stone cheek, shoulder, elbow,
    apples, plums, the faun's hand
  grasping the rigid branch. A third child
  trying to mount a hound's lean back.

162

I pace the pavanne Bernini planned.
I become the marble in his hand.
And I have seen these marble boys before,
cherubs napping in far galleries.
Slack-bellied, bronze, grouped around a tomb,

They wear the same mischief on their lips,
Hinting at their power to undo. The dog
stretches up as the grapes trail down.
A lion's pelt is flung across the trunk.
The boys and faun carouse eternally. My daughter

lengthens into girl and rounds toward wife.
I lose my little beauty by the hour.
I'm past the telling moment of my life.
The marble faun ascends the marble tree.
A lizard suns where everlastings bloom.

Cutting improved the poem. What is left conveys simply and clearly what the earlier draft only hinted at and stumbled around.

In addition to cutting, the poet made other changes. She has reorganized a poem originally arranged by line (a stichic poem) into stanzas. Some of the lines have been moved, from the middle of the poem to the end, for instance. "A child's bottom not quite astride / a hound's lean back" has become "A third child / trying to mount a hound's lean back."

EVERY WORD MUST WORK

Poems are like small rooms. There's no place for clutter. Everything in them must work hard, perhaps doing double or triple duty. In addition to conveying meaning, does the word add to the music of the poem? Does it help build the rhythm or the imagery?

Lawrence Jay Dessner, in his book *How to Write a Poem*, suggests copying each line of your poem over and over, each time leaving out a different word. Try it without the first word, without the second word, and so on.

This is easy on a word processor: just copy the line as many times as there are words in it, and go through each line deleting a different word.

This exercise can be very helpful. It's time consuming, but it will focus your attention on each word. It's a good way to work until you become adept at spotting what needs to be cut.

Using this method, one poet trimmed and shaped the first two lines shown below into the succeeding two lines:

GHAZAL OF THE WORKING MOTHER

Hunting season. In the morning in bed I hear distant guns as hunters aim at deer.

HUNTING SEASON

*Each morning in bed I hear
guns as hunters fire at deer.*

Be sure the words you leave are strong ones, mostly nouns and verbs. And be sure you name what you mean. If you mean *rose*, say *rose*, not *flower*. If you mean *lily*, say *lily*, not *lily-of-the-valley*.

USING ONE WORD INSTEAD OF MANY

Sometimes, it's not a question of removing extra words. You can also replace a string of words with the right word. "A tall yellow flower" might become

"A sunflower." "An orange colored cat" could be a "marmalade cat," or "a ginger cat." "The metal bars on the front of the bike" could be simply "the handlebars." "He had a big long droopy mustache shaped like handlebars" could become "He wore a handlebar mustache."

In a way, you are using shorthand, telegraphing your message to the reader in the fewest possible words. Think of it this way: you are paying for each word—and you want to spend as little as possible. You do pay, of course, not in money, but in lost attention from your reader.

SYNTAX

Do you need every word in a sentence in poetry that you need in prose? No. Sometimes, you don't even need to use a full sentence. You can use fragments—lists of nouns, for instance, or verbs without subjects. If you look hard at every word, you'll see some that can disappear without leaving a trace, leaving the poem better for it.

LOGIC

Finally, look at the order of the elements remaining in your poem. Are the lines in the proper order? Do you tell your story, or paint your picture, logically, so the reader can follow? Sometimes, just rearranging the order of things will allow you to do less explaining.

Some poets, when they reach this stage in revision, type up their poems double-spaced, then cut the lines apart with a pair of scissors. Next, they play with the order of the cut-up lines, physically rearranging them on the page to make sure of the best order. Why not give it a try?

EXERCISE

Take a page of writing—either your own, from a notebook or freewriting session, or a page from a magazine article or newspaper article that captures your imagination. Remove at least half the words, leaving the meaning of the piece unchanged. Don't add anything; just take things out.

To do this, you will need to decide what the piece is about and what the major points are. There are no right answers—only decisions. Keep cutting until what you have left can be arranged into a poem of twenty lines. Make line breaks in appropriate places.

If you do this exercise earnestly, you will learn a great deal about compression. Yes, you will lose nuance. You will lose detail. But you will also convey the main point—whatever you decide that is—more strongly, more quickly.

When in doubt, leave it out.

In general, it takes longer to write the shorter, more densely packed language of poetry. Sometimes, every now and then, it comes easily. Other times, it's hard work.

REVISION

Using the techniques described above, go through your poem, removing any excess language, reordering, rearranging, and filling in better words and additional details where needed.

Type up a clean copy. Make sure to include your name and, if you'd like, the date on which you consider your poem finished.

TWELVE

GOING PUBLIC: CRITIQUES, PUBLICATIONS, READINGS, and CONTESTS

You may write for the joy of it, but the act of writing is not complete in itself. It has its end in its audience.
—Flannery O'Connor

If you have worked through one or more chapters of this book, you now know several ways to look at one of your poems in the process of creation.

If you're lucky enough to be in a writing class, or have a group of friends who are interested in writing and in reading each other's poetry, you can use these same "lenses" to look at poems written by your peers.

SETTING GROUND RULES

If you're in a writing class, your teacher probably has established ground rules for discussing each other's work. If not, or if you're setting up your own group, you might want to consider adopting a set of rules. They needn't be a burden; in fact, they will probably help keep things moving along in a more peaceful and constructive manner.

Group discussion is a useful source of comments, criticisms, and suggestions for a poet.

To begin, agree that you will be discussing the poetry, not the poet. There will be no name-calling, rudeness, or unkindness—no matter what. Writing is self-revelation, and when we reveal ourselves, we make ourselves vulnerable. Poetry groups need to be safe places where people can share their work and get advice and helpful criticism—without fear of personal attack.

Second, it helps to assume that the speaker of the poem is not the writer of the poem. Even if the poem is wildly autobiographical, just pretend the speaker and the poet are somewhat separate. This approach makes it easier for group members to give and receive criticism.

It's much easier for someone to hear, "I think the speaker of this poem is overlooking an important element of the situation," than to hear, "You're being a jerk in this poem." Remember: you are not finding fault with the person who wrote the poem. You are pointing out weaknesses in the work in order to help the writer improve the poem.

Take turns getting attention in the group. Whether you meet every week, every other week, or once a month, make sure each person who has brought writing gets to read it and have it commented upon. Don't send anyone home with unread work.

If people have brought work but are shy about presenting it, it sometimes make sense to insist that everyone must bring writing for discussion every time you meet. That way, everyone will have something at stake.

It also helps if every member of the group has a copy of the poem under discussion to look at and mark up. Hand out all copies at the beginning of each session, so the paperwork is out of the way.

BEGINNING THE SESSION

Have the poet read his or her poem aloud. The poet should not do lengthy introductions. It is not necessary or helpful to explain what the poem is about, how it came to be written, or what it really means.

Nor does it help to be self-deprecating before presentation. "This is really awful—but I didn't have time to revise it," or "I know this is lousy, but…" is no way to introduce a poem. Just read. Let the poem do its work, and see how much or little comes across.

While the poet is reading, the rest of the group should listen intently. During the reading, mark anything that strikes you as wonderful (you might use a plus sign or a star), anything that strikes as awful (use a minus sign or a check), and anything that raises a question (with a question mark).

Once the reading is done, allow a few moments for reflection. During this time—and during the discussion of his or her poem—the poet should be quiet. This is the poet's time to listen, to make notes, to take in what others are saying and thinking and sharing about the work.

SUMMARIZE

It is often helpful to begin discussing an individual poem with a summary: have someone other than the poet say what the poem is about. See if everyone agrees. If not, make certain that all opinions are aired and heard. You don't have to decide on what it means—but the poet should be given the benefit of all the different interpretations.

Other helpful information might arise out of the following kinds of questions:

- How does the poem affect you?
- What is the general feeling, the outline of the story, the poem is trying to convey?
- What feeling does it communicate?
- What words in the poem are working most strongly to communicate this feeling?
- What concrete images that appeal to the senses are there?
- How do they contribute to the overall impression the poet seems to be aiming for?

WHAT'S WORKING?

Next, the group should point to all the positive things in the poem—the parts that you've marked as good.

Let the writer hear what things are working well, what you like about them, why they seem to work. Is the rhythm good? Do you love the word choice, the comparison, the images that are used? Let the poet know.

Once the good news is shared, begin to talk about the things you didn't understand. Raise the questions for the poet: "I didn't get what you meant by 'mold' in the last line," or, "I wasn't sure whether you meant x or y." This is not the time for the poet to answer—but to listen and make notes.

WHAT CAN BE IMPROVED?

Finally, the group should weigh in with their criticisms: what parts of the poem aren't working. You might suggest substitutions, or edits, if you think they will improve the poem. But do not expect the poet to make the changes you suggest. You can offer your opinions; you can't enforce them. Never suggest that a poet take your offering literally and incorporate it into the poem.

When offering critiques, you might use reasons you've learned by reading one or more chapters of this book. Be as specific as you can, telling the poet what you think doesn't work, and why.

It's helpful, for instance, to say things like: "The image in the beginning of the poem seems too abstract." "The rhythm in the middle of the poem is too regular—or irregular." "It's hard for me to see, hear, or feel what's going on in the third stanza."

THE POET'S TURN

When the discussion has run its course—or when the time allotted for discussion is up—let the poet speak. He or she can ask questions now, in order to clarify some issues raised during discussion. Or the poet can talk about the poem and answer questions that were raised.

This is the time for dialogue and comment. Make sure you allow enough time for the poet to get a clear idea of the group's reaction to his or her work and a feeling of satisfaction. It's customary for the poet to thank the group for their comments.

PATIENCE

Learning to be a useful critic takes time. Be patient with yourself and others. And be gentle. Writing poetry is a hard and often lonely task. It's worth taking the time to make sure you don't make enemies of others who are willing to share their work and their insights with you.

PUBLICATIONS

It's exciting to see your work in print. If you have a strong ego, why not send some poems out to be considered for publication?

A strong ego is helpful, because most of your work will be returned. Sometimes, it will be returned with helpful comments, encouragement, or suggestions. More often, it will come back with a printed rejection slip. Occasionally, it will be returned unread.

This generally means very little about the quality of your work. Editors who read poetry submissions are overwhelmed and underpaid. They are doing the best they can. Don't expect them to serve the purpose of a writing group. They won't offer detailed criticism, and if you expect lots of attention from an editor, you are bound to be disappointed.

Getting poems rejected doesn't mean that they are bad or badly written poems. Getting poems accepted and published doesn't even mean they're good. Plenty of bad poems get published. Plenty of good ones languish, unread, for years. Think of Emily Dickinson, writing in her small room simply for the sake of writing and, except for a few poems, unpublished in her lifetime.

SELECTING MAGAZINES

It's best to send your poems to magazines with which you are familiar, and perhaps even to magazines that feature the work of younger writers.

You can use *Poet's Market* to help locate such magazines. Published annually, it lists hundreds of publications, along with what they are looking for, how long they take to respond, and so on.

Once you identify a likely market, it's a good idea to send for a sample copy of the magazine and study it before mailing in your work. Or look for the magazine at your local or school library and read a few issues, just to give yourself an idea of the kind of work it prints.

Some magazines are aimed at teen writers and readers. *Poets & Writers*, on Spring Street in New York City, publishes a list of these. Contact them for more information.

PREPARING POEMS FOR PUBLICATION

Type up or print out your polished poem. In the upper left-hand corner, type your name and address. Then center the poem on the page. Type single- or double-spaced, as you prefer, but only one poem to a page no matter how brief. At the bottom of the poem, type your name.

Prepare an envelope addressed to the magazine. In addition, you may include an envelope addressed to yourself, already stamped, for the return of your work. This is called a self-addressed stamped envelope, or SASE.

If you do not want your poems returned, you can include a postcard, also stamped and addressed to yourself. This will allow the editor to respond quickly to your work.

Send no more than three to five poems to one publisher. One or two is also fine.

You may include a brief, businesslike cover letter addressed to the poetry editor, mentioning a relevant detail or two about yourself. But don't say too much. As in a discussion group, so in an editorial office: if a poem needs too much explanation and set-up, the poem needs revision. Let your poems stand alone.

You can expect to hear from magazines within three months. If three months pass and you have heard nothing, send a postcard inquiring about your work.

SELF-PUBLISHING

Walt Whitman published his own poems. So have many other poets. Since the appearance of the computer and the copy machine, it's easy to publish your own poems, too.

Type up or print out the poems you'd like to publish. Arrange them in a good order. Design a cover. Add a little art work. Take the whole package to a copy center, and *voila!*— you're a published author.

You might do an anthology, including work from your class or informal poetry group. Or set up a zine, including work—poetry, prose, photographs, art, comics—from many friends. Some students produce three or four of these each school year and sell copies in the halls—for fifty cents or a dollar—to their friends and classmates.

READINGS

Once you've put together a collection of your work, even if it's three to five poems, you might want to consider reading some of them to an audience. Many high schools now sponsor poetry readings. Sometimes you have to arrange with a coordinator to get on the program. Other times, the readings are "open mike," and anyone who wants to read may do so.

Obviously, the quality of work that's presented at these readings can vary wildly. But if you want to find an audience for your work, and you are not terribly shy, you might enjoy reading your poems to a group.

Don't read for too long. A few short poems that the audience can grasp and appreciate will have more impact than a long, rambling, boring work.

In addition to readings sponsored by schools, there are many readings given at churches, in coffee-houses, and in bookstores. Many of these series have prescheduled performers, as well as open-mike time. The local Y may have a reading especially for teen writers. Check your local papers and friends who are interested in poetry to find a spot where you can read your work.

CONTESTS

There are two kinds of poetry contests: those designed to foster and reward the writing of poetry, and those designed to make money for the people who run the contest. Many contests are listed in publications such as *Poets & Writers*, and advertisements for poetry contests appear in many newspapers and general interest magazines.

How can you tell which kind of contest is which? In general, contests that pay you money for winning

*A group of young people enthusiastically discusses
a speaker's work at a local poetry reading.*

are better than contests that require you to pay for entering and winning. The Poetry Society of America, for example, runs an annual contest for student poets. The PSA also runs other reputable poetry contests. Some are limited to PSA members, and there is no entry fee. Others are also open to non-members, who must pay a small entry fee. The poetry contest for high school students is free to enter. The prize is one hundred dollars, and an opportunity to read your poem at an awards ceremony, usually held in New York City.

Other contests are less reputable. One publisher advertises early and often, enticing poets with large cash prizes. Enter, and more than likely, at least one of your poems will be accepted. If you want them to include any information about you, however, known as contributor's notes, you will need to pay approximately twenty dollars. And if you want to see your poem in print, you will need to pay far more. Some of their volumes cost as much as seventy dollars.

You will have to decide whether publication in such a volume is worth such a hefty investment. In deciding, you might consider several factors:

First, these volumes have no prestige among serious poets, who know them for what they are.

Second, how many copies of your poem, or collection of poems, could you "publish" for that money? How many books of poetry could you buy? How many subscriptions to little magazines that publish interesting verse? How many stamps and envelopes with which to send your work to serious, respectable markets?

Poetry does not, for the most part, pay. On the other hand, you've invested your time, your thought, your energy and talent and creativity and craft. Do you really want to pay to see it in print, too?

FOR FURTHER READING

Behn, Robin, and Twitchell, Chase, editors. *The Practice of Poetry: Writing Exercises From Poets Who Teach* (New York: HarperCollins, 1992).

Bishop, Elizabeth. *The Complete Poems: 1927–1979* (New York: Farrar Straus Giroux, 1983).

Cameron, Julia. *The Artist's Way: A Spiritual Path to Higher Creativity* (New York: G.P. Putnam's Sons, 1992).

Fussell, Paul. *Poetic Meter and Poetic Form* (New York: Random House, 1965).

Goldberg, Natalie. *Writing Down the Bones* (Boston: Shambhala Publications, Inc., 1986).

Dacey, Philip and Jauss, David, editors. *Strong Measures: Contemporary American Poetry in Traditional Forms* (New York: Random House, 1983).

Mendelstam, Nadezhda. *Hope Against Hope: A Memoir* (New York: Atheneum, 1970).

Miller, Brett C. *Elizabeth Bishop: Life and the Memory of It* (Berkley: University of California Press, 1993).

Nims, John Frederick. *Western Wind: An Introduction to Poetry* (New York: Random House, 1983).

Packard, William, ed. *The Craft of Poetry: Interviews from the New York Quarterly* (New York: Doubleday & Co., 1974).

Padgett, Ron. *The Teachers and Writers Handbook of Poetic Forms* (New York: Teachers and Writers Collaborative, 1987).

Plimpton, George, ed. *Poets at Work: The Paris Review Interviews* (New York: Penguin Books, 1984).

Pound, Ezra. *The ABC of Reading* (New York: New Directions Paperback, 1960).

Turco, Lewis. *The Book of Forms* (New York: E.P. Dutton & Co., 1968).

Ueland, Brenda. *If You Want to Write* (St. Paul: Graywolf Press, 1987).

Magazines

Poets & Writers Magazine, Poets and Writers, 72 Spring Street, New York, NY 10012.

> Interviews with poets and writers, articles by editors, lists of grants, awards, and deadlines, as well as advertisements from publishers seeking poems for magazines, chapbooks, and anthologies.

Writes of Passage: The Literary Journal for Teenagers, P.O Box 7676, Greenwich, CT 06836.

> Publishes poetry and prose by teenagers, as well as features such as "Tips and Advice on Getting Published."

Organizations

Poetry Society of America, 15 Gramercy Park, New York, NY 10003.

> Membership dues begin at $25.00 per year for students. Sponsors annual poetry awards, including the Louise Louis/Emily Bourne Student Poetry Award; $100 for the best unpublished poem by a high school or prepatory school student (grades 9 to 12) from the United States. Membership is not necessary to enter this contest.

INDEX

E

Eady, Cornelius, 97
Ellington, Duke, 95
Elliott, George G., 25
emotion. *See* feeling
"Emperor of Ice Cream,
    The," 144
Empires, 147
English sonnet, 120
enjambment, 141
"Epistle to Dr. Arbuthnot," 102
"Essay on Criticism," 92
"Evangeline," 103
"Eve of Saint Agnes," 61, 64
expression, 19
eye rhyme, 88–89

F

feeling, 10, 20, 23, 33, 41,
    83, 113, 170
    importance of, 24
    reality of, 24
feet, 100–103, 104, 110
Fermat, Pierre de, 31
figurative language,
    68–80, 86
figures of speech.
    See figurative language
"First Lesson," 39–40
first draft. *See* draft, first
"Fish, The," 48, 53
"Foot, The," 33
Forché, Carolyn, 28
form. *See* poetry, forms of
free verse, 18, 108, 111,
    112, 137–138
    line, the, 138–139
    line breaks, 139–141
    sound of, 142
    word choices, 141
    writing in, 142
freewriting, 28–29, 30,
    151–152
"Frog in the Swimming Pool,
    The," 33
Frost, Robert, 18, 23, 65, 68,
    81, 104–105, 138, 144

Fuller, Dr., 81
Fussell, Paul, 23, 24, 95, 112

G

genre, 22
"Ghazal of the Working
    Mother," 164
Ginsberg, Allen, 113, 138,
    142, 150–151
Glück, Louise, 45, *46*,
    141, 143
Goldberg, Natalie, 27–28
Guest, Edgar, 97
"Gulliver," 75

H

haiku, 115
half rhyme, 86, 87.
    See also off rhyme
hearing, 61. *See also* senses
heptameter, 104
Herbert, George, 60
heroic couplets, 106, 108
hexameter, 104
Hikmet, Nazim, 25, 39
Hollander, John, 60, 108
homonyms, 135
Horace, 23, 159
How to Write a Poem, 164
Howard, Richard, 23
Hughes, Ted, 38, 44
"Hunting Season," 164

I

"I Wandered Lonely as a
    Cloud," 61
"I Was on a Golf Course the
    Day John Cage Died of a
    Stroke," 33
iambic meter, 97, 98, 101,
    102, 109, 110, 111, 123
iambic pentameter,
    105–108, 120, 124, 125,
    158, 159
ideas, 20, 56, 58
If You Want to Write, 28
imagery, 86, 163

ACKNOWLEDGEMENTS

The following publishers have generously given permission to use extended quotations from the following copyrighted works: From *Ariel* by Sylvia Plath. Copyright 1965 by Ted Hughes. Reprinted by permission of HarperCollins Publishers. From *A Writer's Time* by Kenneth Atchity. Copyright 1988 by Kenneth Atchity. Reprinted by permission of W.W. Norton & Company. From "The Mind is an Enchanting Thing" by Marianne Moore. Copyright 1944 by Marianne Moore and renewed 1972 by Marianne Moore. Reprinted with permission by Simon & Schuster from *The Collected Poems of Marianne Moore*. From *The Kingfisher* by Amy Clampitt. Copyright 1983 by Amy Clampitt. Reprinted by permission of Alfred A. Knopf Inc. From *ABC of Reading*. Copyright 1934 by Ezra Pound. Reprinted by permission of New Directions Publishing Corp. From *The Poems of Dylan Thomas* by Dylan Thomas. Copyright 1952 by Dylan Thomas. Reprinted by permission of New Directions Publishing Corp. From *Pairs* by Philip Booth. Copyright 1994 by Philip Booth.

ABOUT THE AUTHOR

Margaret Ryan works as a speechwriter for a major corporation. She has also published two books of poetry and is the author of *How to Give a Speech*, published by Franklin Watts. Ms. Ryan makes her home in New York City with her husband and daughter.